Algebra of Night

New & Selected Poems   1948-1998

Algebra of Night

New & Selected Poems   1948-1998

WILLIS BARNSTONE

The Sheep Meadow Press
Riverdale-on-Hudson, New York

All inquiries and permission requests should be addressed to:
The Sheep Meadow Press
PO Box 1345
Riverdale-on-Hudson, NY 10471

Designed by S.M.
Distributed by Unversity Press of New England.

Printed on acid-free paper in the United States. This book meets the
guidelines for permanence and durability of the Committee on
Production Guidelines for Book Longevity of the Council on Library
Resources.

ISBN 1-878818-60-0

Some of these poems have appeared in the following publications:

Agni, The Age of Koestler, The American Scholar, The American Voice, The Antioch Review, The Arizona Quarterly, Boundary 2, Ballantonian, The California Quarterly, The Chelsea Review, The Chicago Review, Choice, The Colorado Quarterly, Columbian University Forum, Correspondences, CutBank, Denver Quarterly, Exquisite Corpse, The Field Museum of Natural History Bulletin, The Formalist, Holiday, The Indiana Sesquicentennial Poets, Indiana Writes, International Poetry Review, In the Midst of Winter: Selections from the Literature of Mourning, Ion, Kayak, The Journal of the Hellenic Diaspora, The Kenyon Review, The Literary Review, The Madison Review, The Massachusetts Review, The Modern Poetry Review, Mundus Artium, The Nation, New Campus Writing, New Letters, New Orlando Poetry, The New Republic, The New York Quarterly, Nimrod, The North American Review, The Notre Dame Review, The New Yorker, The Northwest Review, La Opinión (Buenos Aires), *The Partisan Review, The Paris Review, Poetry Flash, Poetry Now, Points* (Paris), *Prairie Schooner, Quarterly West, The Sewanee Review, The Southern Poetry Review, The Southern Review, Stoney Lonesome, The Tar River Review, The Times Literary Supplement, The Translatlantic Review, Triad, Voices within the Ark: Modern Jewish Poets, La Voz, The Wesleyan Cardinal, The Wisconsin Review, The Yale Review.*

I wish to thank the publisher Stanley Moss for suggesting this volume and for being patient for several years while I worked on it. I am grateful to Michael Lowenthal and Philip Pachota of the University Press of New England for making possible the publication of *The Secret Reader*. Reflecting eighteen years of writing and tinkering, it is the core selection in this book. Among many who have read, made suggestions, and stood near are Gerald Stern, Ayame Fukuda, Shanon Doyne, Sarah Handler, Helle Tzalopoulou Barnstone, and my children Aliki, Robert, and Tony.

for

Aliki
Robert
Tony

Contents

Poems of Exchange 1951

White Weathercock

A coquette wind blows
A white weathercock
In a hollow
Deep in me.

The weathercock
In unmoving flight
Scrapes the hollow
Deep and empty.

A woman's breath
Moves the white cock
Swinging inward outward
Outward inward

In unmoving flight.
The vane points only one way
And never back
From where it came.

Bodies in Mexico City, 1947

Mounds of legs at midnight,
The night a lunatic of ice:
White cement of the street,
Wild children of nothing.

The orphans to keep warm
On Avenida Juan Delatrán
Are piled on each other
Like stacks of used tires.

Who are these children
Who sleep in the street?

All the doors are soiled
The wall posters are mute;
Windows are tongueless,
The night without ears.

Night is a lunatic of ice
Without future or past.
The brats of the moon
Are asleep in the street.

Who are these children
Who sleep in the street?

Christmas Night After the Civil War, 1949

In their striped Sunday-best rags
Three musicians from the north

Are waiting by our city door
On the big marble landing.

We let them in to play.
A cloudy Sunday after the war,

Athens white with rare snow
Concealing the bullet holes,

Three cold musicians are playing
Through the Christmas night.

Each wears a moon-gray shirt
Over a cracked poor-man's torso.

The singer lacks two fingers,
The clarino player is blind,

The violinist has one good leg.
Grave peasants sing Byzantine carols

Rolling hoarsely through the frost.
We eat cucumbers and moon cheese

And dance on Thracian rugs.
When they do an island song

Their passion never stops.
Trailing them, we traipse out

Into the street, dance on snow,
Ouzo in hand, and dish out

Drachmas, which they pocket
Unsmiling as they walk away.

End of the Greek War

for Vicente Aleixandre

In a dark pool hall
              ghosts sip sweet coffee.

An amputee smokes
              whistles as he eyeballs

And shoots for the pocket
              He wins an ouzo,

Hops outside to the
              king's park of Zappeion

Where sun falls in the still
              rooms of a bird's ear,

But no one walks
                    on the marble ghost on the hill.

The abandoned Parthenon
                    is sleepy.

I meander a bit
                    on cloudy sand

Out to olive groves
                    who wrestle an ax.

Herons rise in a terror
                    from the big guns.

Cemetaries cannot
                    care about the dead

Or feel the dark drum
                    in the cypresses.

The dead talk about
                    but fail to show.

The amputee strolls
                    twirling worry beads

And wearing a carnation
                    in his kouros lips

All morning in memory
                    of hostages in trucks.

Dinner in the Only-for-Sunday Living Room

Commonly we eat at the long table
Crowding the narrow kitchen. Honey, lemons,
    peeling knives,
A pitcher of water and retsina always on the cloth.
My Greek family and I speak Greek and French
Except when our blond peasant cousin Xanthí
(Who was kidnaped in civil war to haul weapons
And food on her back like a donkey
Till she escaped) comes down from the mountains
    for a visit.
But tonight is December, holidays,
And Vassíli my father-in-law made a delicious vassilópita
    egg bread.
He cooks so he can know how
To treat his patients he says. At dessert the suspense
Is unbearable. The one who is youngest
Or luckiest is supposed to get
The slice with the English gold pound coin hidden
    in the cake.
We dig in and I almost break my tooth.

Below the Sanatorium

The men with tuberculosis like to stroll
Down from the sanatoriums
Near the top of marble Mount Pendeli

And sometimes smoke Papastrátos 1,
Quietly, in light autumn clothes.
I stroll with them, fresh from

Olives and a roll-and-feta breakfast
Until the Stasis[1] where I hop the bus
To work. It is at a small academy

For Konstantinos, the king's son,
Who is nine. One of the pupils
(Whose father lost his arms in Albania)

Yells: "Your Highness, I'll bust your face,
Ta moutrasou,[2] if you don't get your ass
Over here and boot the ball!"

At twenty-one I'm a French teacher.
Dáskalos,[3] they call me. After classes
I trudge home up the night-scented tar road,

Moon under my sneakers, talking
About monarchy to the patients,
Who sleep up in the clinics. "You're free,"

the men in pajamas say. Back at school
lunch, I spar with the queen. At the year's end
I am fired and go to an island.

---

[1] Stop

[2] Your snout

[3] Teacher

From This White Island   1960

An Island

By white walls and scent of orange leaves,
  I know nothing and the planet blurs.
    By this sea of squid and dolphins
I see but fish in a dome of sun.

In stars that nail me to a door
  There are women with burning hair,
    And on the quay at night I feel
But hurricanes and rigid dawn.

On cobblestones at day I watch
  Some crazy seabirds fall and drown
    And as the bodies sink to sand
I know I pay my birth with death.

I only see some plains of grass
  And sky-sleep in the crossing storks.
    I know nothing and see but fire
In the vocano of a cat's eye.

The Small White Byzantine Chapel

On this island nude and nearly treeless
But for the few acacia trees in bloom
In the small white plazas of stone and sun

With their zones of salt and seaweed aroma,
On the far side across the island rock
And the dry wind and fresh donkey dung,

The cupola of the white chapel stares:
A stucco eyeball brightening the sky.
Inside are sparks and fumes of incense

And candle flames before the iconostasis
Where a slant-eyed Virgin leans in grief:
O points of mystery in the finite space!

Outside, the priest's mad daughter smokes
And curses as she heads for the windmills.
In black air within the whitewashed dome

The priest with a bad heart sings like a bird
Floating high in the smoky firmament.
O lifelong darkness in the finite vault

As the white dome vainly searches the sky.

Waiting in the Port Café, 1950

Go now to this wondrous island.
Find the pepper tree where your dream
Hammers lightning in the blue leaves.
Sleep with an honest whore and know
The woman's love, her nightly rise.
Go quickly to this wondrous island
And chew the apple, lick the sap
And suck the fire in the olive heart.
Walk barefoot in this wondrous port,
For sun will darken in your chest
And sea spread blackly through your feet.
The sea will blacken all of space,
And you, a pin, will fall and fall.

Now

Be still. Be still. Open your eyes
Like still sails in a constant wind,
And let the black glass of thought cloud
The daylit picture in your eyes:
let the center dull the icon,
Shield and still the bright illusion, now.
And see, now, with your pupils wide
Like the planet's unbound air, see
Your strength and sudden ocean flights
Behind the simple lens of sight—
Be still. Be still. Open your eyes
While skies lacquer into rimless night.

Kyrie Babi, Beggar Musician from Anatolia, Sitting on Pendeli Road with His Braille Bible

Kyrie Babi's scooped-out eyeballs are gone
And watery sockets scar his baby face
With sewn-up holes of Bible light.

Glory burns inside, yet the devil's close
And the devil's friends—who make him trip and fall—
Will grovel in the burning grease of hell.

Cats and dogs are bearded brats of Christ.
All love God. Babi loves every simple being,
And he'd fondle lambs, bears, tigers, lions,

Any furry felted hide or flying thing.
Kyrie Babi's fingers, firebirds in black space,
Love to rest on necks of donkeys eating grass.

The lily spins. Babi talks of death. He's sick.
He cannot swallow. Pus and tonsillitis.
He wipes his hot face with a wasted hand.

He takes a step and stumbles in a furrow.
Wanting life and warmth and loving brothers,
He founders in a ditch of carbon daisies.

The blindman's sockets feel a blow of light
And yellow angels plummet through his sleep,
His agony, and death comes cheap with peace.

Island Monastery

In the glass desert of an asphodel,
In sunflowers by the fertile sea,
In the nude black flesh of an olive,
I have found a monastery.

I roam the patio garden,
I hear a hill river in the large bell.
Under a pure blue cape of sky
I am not walled in by sheer walls.

Behind my eyes is desolation,
Yet near me grows a cypress,
A brown flower drunk on raki.
Behind my eyes are black spaces.

I roam the patio garden
(there is sun on the peaceful trees)
And step within my barren mind
Down in flight to a sea on fire.

Vert-le-Petit

The bright cuckoo bird reaches out
On castle France spring morning,
And apple trees of Vert-le-Petit
Send away white sobs of beauty
And feed us with a mystic bread.

Then male smell of ox fills our nostrils.
Our love washes through us and we quiver
In the green waves growing hot and cold,
In the turfy furrows where our bodies
Hug the ivory of the young earth.

Chips of stars hum behind the daylight
And black-eyed pansies in their yellow folds
Holds the pricked air on golden spots.
We refuse to wake and sunlight swims
Below our eyelids as a warm-water fish.

Negro castillo

Por la ventana redonda
del cuerpo, negro castillo,
el ave de la negrura
ya sale buscando el día.
Busca la sombra del mar
en donde rondan los peces,
y la arena, blanda arena,
donde su perfil descansa.

Pájaro de la negrura,
¿qué es este grito penoso
que alumbra toda la playa?

Queman las velas del cielo
en aire y sol bondadoso.

El pájaro no responde
por ser animal agudo,
y busca siempre más sol,
aspirando al mediodía.
Espera cambiar su cuerpo
por el brillo de cenizas.

Un pájaro calcinado
vuelve a la negra ventana.
Antes era palomica
con alas de blanca paz.
Ahora vuela invisible,
rayo de luna borrada.

Ansía cual niño ciego
un farol en el castillo.
Fuera, luce la negrura;
dentro, un amor sin objecto.
Mas sólo el amor clarea
en el castillo la sombra.

A Fly

On this hot day of rain my body walks
In sweaty clothes with cuffs rolled at the elbow.
Dreaming beyond the view where its eyes balk,
A fly, trapped, bangs at space beyond the window.
Apathy. Habitude. Even the weather
Puts the fire out. The daily this and that
Calms my hill horse, confining it in leather
And tames the moon, the nightly acrobat.
The humid sunrays seethe inside my flesh.
I see no dome of light, no diamond beach,

No holy God to halt the minute gun,
Yet like the fly buzzing against the mesh
My body feels the sky it cannot reach
And craves for darkness in the alien sun.

Mother Disappears

While you are lowered in the clay
We watch under the summer sun.
The rocking of the coffin done,
Our meager party goes away.
You left so quickly for the night
Almost no one on the great earth
Observes the moment of your death.
We few who knew your quiet light
Try to remember, yet forget,
And neither memory nor talk
Will bring you sun once it has set.
Your life was brief—a morning walk.
We whom you loved still feel an O
Of quiet absence in Maine snow.

Middletown Children

After the winter freeze,
Sweet sun lies on the sidewalk, on the walls,
On my muddy shoes, on black spongy ground
Not quite green but finally warm.

The grass in the small town's
Graveyard begins to blade again around
The useless gate and on the shallow mounds
marking the children's plots.

That smell of earth and lilac
Wavers with the pigeons in a slow wind
That rings the violet bells of irises
        And spins the dust around new weeds.

        The cemetery slabs
Are one hundred years above the small mounds,
And one now can recall those children
        Who smell of earth and lilac.

A Girl in a Coma in the Cancer Ward at the Nun's Hospital in Perigueux

Through bright air above the Dordogne valley,
A sunny and womanly soft meadow of castles,

Morning light passes through tall glass walls
And spreads like cotton cloth in the corridors.

The hospital receives the daylight as a blessing,
Its modern rooms lit with a happier cleanness

Enveloping the children from the Perigord
Whose ravaged bodies linger in daytime sleep.

The nuns like white clouds hover near a child
As her breathing weakens on this full morning.

She is unknowing as we what the light means,
Why she must disappear so soon in the earth.

Sunlight reaches through glass walls to her bed,
Sunrays quiver on the sheet drawn near her chin.

Her room high on the soft and unfeeling hill
Is filled with radiance of an almost joyful light.

Poplar Trees Weep Amber

We all want to love her,
And I'd give my right arm
If I could love her deeply,
Yet she walks among us
And I turn the other way.

Clouds burn with sunny gulls,
Lone caïques stroke the sea
And poplar trees weep amber.
I sleep with knife in hand,
She turns the other way.

She is strong as my cold grief,
Swift to love as a queen bee,
I mutilate her body,
Yet I would give my right arm
If I could love her deeply.

She walks near us each day,
Burning gulls screech with joy,
And she would die for me
And bloom life before my eyes
If I could bear to love her.

Light and Darkness

> Once past Acheron, the river of darkness,
> we shall lie as bones and dust.
> —Asklepiades

I wake. Seabirds wheel overhead.
The day shines like a violet grape
In the rose sky of my eyelids.
Sleeping on a Nova Scotia rocky
Beach, I wake with terror and light.
Am I here? I will not be.

One day I will sink into dark,
Down in the very bottom sea
Where now I watch islands of light
And sun shuddering in tall grass.
Just before I open my eyes
I see a vast meadow of rays.

Far in the bay a yellow sail
Looms and blurs in confusing glare.
I think of ancient Greek poets
Who cursed the tomb and praised sweet sun.
Halfway through life, briefly blind,
I think, is this all? Who am I?

Atlantic Coast, Afterward

After the hurricane
There is no time but now.
The beach is a white plane,
The ocean an orange

Leaf upon a blue branch.
Low waves enmesh the sun
And spray it on the sand.
Space and separation.

Gulls by the surf. Green gulls
In a herd and shrill screams.
No. No sound or echo
But single harmonies.

Across the vast beach, light
Diffuses in sober squares.
In a blue plane a boat
Moves far out on its oars.

The Moon's Image

The same moon in Lapland or Almuñécar
stuns with Roman aqueducts and black castanets
and her stone mirror tells nothing.
—Tomasa de la Tienda del Sol

She rose like a yellow buffoon
Over barren plains and a pine tree.
She came over the mountain grass
Like the green horse of the fairy tale,
And stared startled as she looked up
From the blue pool under her feet
Where she was drinking from childhood.

No cry was deep as our insane soul
That tried to know what she was.
No woman was naked as she.

She crossed the horizon as a white ship
Cargoed with brass or slid into the sky,
A red sword cutting the calyx of orchids.
She was a virgin and hurled her kisses
To the nipples of our glowing bodies.
From the center of the dome she glared
With the teeth of a deathless she-wolf.

We ached to read our ultimate image.
She gave us word of our borrowed dust.

She was cold, extreme, and powerful
As she leaned on her highest tower.
She was cruel and unconcerned
As her snow tossed anguish to earth.
Nothing was deeper than her glazed eye
As she laughed like a serene actor
At our certain death before knowledge.

She was the theater of our soul
On which she scratched our image.

We were illiterate and ached to hear.
No woman was naked as she.

Little Girl of Milk

Aliki in Her Crib (Eight Weeks)

Little girl of milk,
    In your sleep you soar
Across the planets with the eye
Of the spotted sandpiper bird,
            Exploring inland streams
            In the universe.

        The North Star is just
            Beyond your fingertips,
And you reach to seize the tiny light
And place it with the dolls and clown
            On the white carpet
            Of the world below.

        When you wake to day
            And the blanket house,
The white paper of your waking mind
Is marked with large fumbling objects,
            And you shut your eyes
            And stretch your feeling arms.

        In the dark, dark era
            Before your screaming birth,
Your kicks were not these giant step
Across the easy beams of stars,
            And their daywhite light,
            Little girl of milk.

Antijournal 1968

God

They made me.
Gave me a white hippy beard
And my throat sang
A loud cuckoo and the godly nightingale
And they heard.

I was a star
In the morning of their book,
A fly at noon,
A beast in their chest, angel in their ribs,
A purple hat.

I was king,
Sun, frog, a lily that lived
In the winter.
They wouldn't let me die amid the murder
From the clocks.

I was a bell,
A cowbell and clavier. At dawn
My whole light
Woke the bubble of the earth, burned its edge,
Blew me inside!

They made me
And unmade me. My best friends
Left. I hang
Around the old neighborhood, lonely man
Behind the times.

My good friends
Suffer for truth. I was their face,
Their joyful lie.
They need me. I make their day ridiculous
And cast them

Alone in the dark.
I was a morning star. Now
I'm nothing. Zero.
They've got nothing like me. Before I left
I made Hell.

U L
F   L
M   N
O O

As a white dome in a romantic eye
I've had my day.
Soon
They will know me,
Explore each contour of my dusty body.

My people no longer bring figs and milk
When they lie down
Deep
In mountain grass.
Only a few still glare at my white thigh.

But I am good. Honeycomb. Meadow of light,
And you can feed
On
My massive shape,
Which can plunge into your eye! I am still

A woman to floor you. An electric bulb,
I can turn off,
On,
Or dance my beam,
The one huge female belly drinking you.

The Fly

I
Am a
Dog of the skies
And food
To

A
Spider.
Even unseen
I buzz
In

A
Nonspace
Of boring time.
Kill me
Or

Be
My host,
I multiply
Like a
Plot

Of
Poison
Ivy. My 6 legs
Crawl your
Dream

Deep
Like oil
In a crankcase.
I stick
My

Noise
In your
Glass ear, break up
Far small
Nerves.

Blake
Had good
Innocent words
For keep-
ing

Me
Alive
And yogis try
Not to
Wipe

Me
Out. All
Life is holy,
Even
Mine.

So
I am
Existence. Me
Too, I
Say,

I
Sip snot,
Am fire at dawn
And fly
Each

Day
To prick
A young girl's nose
When she
Dies.

The Man in the Mirror

While I shave I talk to myself out loud
    Like solitary Indians in Chile
    In the bottom hills of the south.
It makes me nervous to look at that face,
    Which I stare at with eyes of some

One else. On the mirror I keep a poem
    Which keeps slipping into the sink.
    It elates me to work on it,
To pencil the wet page with a far hope
    Of salvation through soapy words.

I talk out loud while drops of blood appear
    On the mirrored face. A bad surgeon.
    And only right now while I talk
Have I any real self. I can hear it
    Like a paper bird in my chest.

These crazy things I do easily.
    It is natural for me to yearn,
    To look at the bulb and see God
Hanging like a carnival star in the air,
    Or fly impossibly to one

I love. The other mask of a calm man
    Takes my whole strength. I can fake it
    And must, but here alone in the bath
I talk to myself and avoid that face
    Which knows me and laughs at a fool.

Evening of a Madman

In black night an egret floats up
                    Like a white lantern
And wind talks through the gusty cracks
          Of the living room.
          I talk to myself loud

And no one on this planet hears.
                    I am alone.
One day down along the Dead Sea
                    I walked in the minerals
          Almost drowning in mud

On a bromide shore. If I sank,
                    That beach of acid
Would not change. I babble as if
                    Someone hears! It means
          As much as traffic lights

In the big world. Can you hear me?
                    You? I think I am
Chatting as I scratch an old sore.
                    No friend exists,
          No love or stranger close.

In the night my mind floats out of
                    Its pocket and sees
Itself. A sweet explosion laughs.
                    So far alone!
          Next life, I'll hear you speak.

A Night on Earth   *1975*

At night

At night I slip out of my bed
and climb into the furnace.
It is not lit and I stretch out
down on the iron floor.
There must be a reason
my calm face blends with soot, and my organs
rage with a great red
luminosity that blackens all the big windows.
I stretch out on the iron floor. Listen to me.
I won't move out of this blasting light.
Let me ask a question.

The noise

The noise of my breath when I sit
absolutely still
resounds like a motor. Then all
the racket of night
is loud. Even my scratching pen
echoes like pouring cement.
When I sit still I hear the world
pounding outside. In me
it also pounds. It wants to get
out. A panther sees bars
and bars. It sings. In the zoo
I begin to scream.

Antonio

Antonio is my poet. Machado
the big sloppy Sevillano,
grave as a dying child and funny
like a bright orange. He
never yells or weeps or makes up
a thing. But he lives in
a dreaming stork, a hill or poplar
or in his far Chinese love
whom he meets only a few times
when lightning fills his room.
A mountain burns in him, and lonely
Antonio walks in blue
lands and sun, in the dream and wheat
of childhood. He is so
grave with round feeling, no one is
as quiet as deep Machado.

Aliki in the woods

We invented a book, you and I
in luminous woods. The tulip trees
were starfish on fire, and black oaks
your blue alarm clock that sang in wonder
as we fought like drowning cats about
the good sun. We walked at rainy dawn
and you told me how you cared for mice
and icky frogs. Then the dawn got mad.
I took you to our barn. With a pen
you drew a bed of luminous trees.

Banishment

As usual I wake up in my country
but I am in exile
and know nothing about a bloody prison fight
during the carnival in Vera Cruz
where an Indian in his white cotton huipil
is ripped apart with a machete from anus to throat.
Yet I smell the blood on the Indianapolis wall
and watch the brown child with her swollen belly
sitting with flies. That knowledge
is mine. I have always been comfortably banished
with the dispossessed, the filthy,
the poor, the murdered, the suicide
for whom my heart stays open
like an eye during a rain storm.

Near a Buenos Aires Book Store

I dream with you through the loud night
of guerrilla strikes in Córdoba,
and at the big naval base at La Plata.
In the streets the police in fat boots
knock on doors. The young are drugged,
put in small planes and dropped in

the Rio de la Plata. They search men
and women, hands against the wall.
I stood unable to speak near a pasta shop
and a rare book store with sepia engravings
of battles in the Crimea as they tossed
a young woman in their car trunk.

I dream with you through the night.
You are beautiful in the shadows

of clouds over the bay, the mouth
of an enormous river of the Dirty War.
Under searchlights in Plaza de Mayo
I explore you, possess you, hug the dream

over the street where the café explodes
and we dance glad and dumbly tumbling
like acrobats into arenas of light.
Our warm arms lock at the fingertips
until shadows wash into high morning
and the fitful concussion of the bombs.

Lapland

The roots of the earth protrude
down into the pinegray ocean
and up into the glacial snow.

There are not many fir trees
as we push into the unreal
north. We are beyond the green

and on nude scrubby earth again.
Here where snow yawns into the
sea, and air is clean like fish,

distance and form and seasons
are more true than the odd boat
or village. Time. This land is

dream—planet where almost no one
is—or if real, then quick cities
south are dream before the slow

iceland. At night sunshine floats
on big mountain ribs of snow;
gulls cry and cod run in the ocean.

Christmas on Plato Street

Suddenly outside the door in the morning
by the dusty plane trees,
five orphans tap a steel triangle
and sing about Saint Basil who is coming,
he is coming
from southern Turkey with gifts
and the bright lead of salvation.
Their eyes are black eggs gazing up
to Attic heaven
with the boredom of an ancient monk
chanting in his cell on the Holy Mountain,
But they are not the mysterious troupe
with exquisite music passing through Alexandria's
ancient alleys
out to the city gate the night before the battle.
The five orphans stand
by the seated eggman gossiping, playing dominoes
and clacking beads
in front of the butcher shop
where an unfrosted 200 watt bulb outside
burns like a marble Apollo.

Birthplace

When we return the house is sold,
                              but the bishop oaks
and princess maples still lay shadows on the lawn,
and chestnut trees along the sloping street
smell of red Fall,
                              and nuts and wingseeds
caped the red-brick walks.

Around the town
                              The air is clean with pines
and sudden lakes around the rocky potato farms,

and twenty miles away the ocean moves
down from the arctic, dragging chunks of ice.

The soil has a sweet acid smell where time
began.
                    The planet shone with light
one morning on a winter hill in Maine,
and light will glow until my eyes congeal
and town and sun explode around my corpse.

Beast in the Attic

I kill a wasp and go back to my chair.
Now there is only me
                              and a few words
I drool about the agony of truth.

Today spring is an orchard
                              of unreality
with so much yellow
                              in the air
and the corpse of a bug is nothing
when hysteria
                    a jackal in my shoes
lies only a sock away.
Is it true I'm here?
                    Or who is the madman
shivering to come up
                    under my breath
and burn out the hive with kerosene

or rock a yellow dogwood

                    over a cliff?

In a wad of cream

                a wasp lies remote
unimportant on the glass.
Fire is buzzing.
The yellow sky spins like an obsession.

Leap from the Gargoyle

In the ceremony of the sleep of life,
a massive sleep,
I'm tossing around in dirty sheets,

but in the glove of darkness, dark globe,
I may wake up
a while as someone else, and if the blow

of waking doesn't slip me into full
extinction, I
may smell the night of the ecstatic sun

in a pause of falling and floating up,
like that first day,
naked, under lights I never know.

I black out spinning down, or else creep
to the steeple-
edge of madness, and leap from the gargoyle

down to a floating nightmare, and lie quartered
in the air far
away from me, a key dangling in space!

I, W.B.

I ride my blue bike to work
down a potted black alley,
a shallow scholar and a minor poet.

In the wire cage I carry
the Song of Songs—my latest love—
and hear the coeds sigh as they screw

in barely furnished pads.
I don't even have a beard
to show. I live a bit on home, a few beers

and what the others tell me.
My soul feeds on foreign flicks
or loneliness, terror, and a flirting pit

of light. A loner among friends,
at night I take a sleeping pill
that wakes me up to dream and dream.

Against W.B.

My friends say to me I talk too much
or show my poems cheaply to anyone
or am still a child.

They couldn't hurt me if they were wrong,
and bats who wander in my sleep
dive at me with me,

my chatter and stunts—all facts and proof
of guilt. And when they tell me, I know
deep down they are right,

down in the belly where the tense child
wants to explore and scream what he feels.
I loudly accuse

my mouth, and say it's time to become
a man. Yet sly I am a man
or a savage child.

Flashing Beams

I watch the river flashing dark
and white and gloom, electric white, white and
I feel the ocean widening into sun,
then gloom, and a childhood blackened
by sudden fury in my parents' stark
struggles that are never won.

Our bedroom on the second floor
eyes the raw park and its congealing wind.
The river like a valley of forged iron
is cut and raked by disciplined
neon signs flashing on the Jersey shore.
Occasionally a siren

rings inhuman pleas through the cold:
an ambulance down a back street. In front
a blue policeman clubs a row of trees.
Through the blue window slips a blunt
sword of icy air. All the older household
is asleep. On my knees

gloomily I see a tugboat flare,
foghorn cries, a boat glides like a dirty ghost.
I hear their threats of suicide, the screams,

You goddam bitch! With a bed-post
my brother clubs me. I love them all but fear
the darkening of the beams.

Rainy Sunday

You are not here and I turn more alive
and dark. I am with those of little faith,
fearing you will step out of focus. But

you are real, dropping your red dress by a
bed. I look at a huge blowup of you
taped on the door (you tried to maltreat it

with a stick-on moustache) and the truth is
your mind, which I hear like the clock outside
telling me I should take my Fiat home

and learn to sleep. I feel the nowness as
if the thought in me fell away, as if
nothing were inside my skin. I lose touch

with consciousness, a man of little faith,
and immediately you have come back
where no one seems to be, and my belly

wakes, shuddering near your belly, and milk
of communion peaks through us, raising us
as a single astronaut to restaurants

of heaven with unusual names, where
over a candle and lentils you speak
about untrapped women. Woman of deep

fear against the scattering of lambs,
fearless before thugs, quick-brained as a fish
nine fathoms down, when you appear my church

is jammed. A week of drizzle and I'm dark
for you, but scarcely terrified with you
inside my skin. Peace comes with illusion,

you are real, dropping your dress. I drink
orange juice for joy and morning. I'm with you.
If one owns two shirts give away a rose.

From a Blue House

My poet friends always save me. Pedro
Salinas, when I fumbled at night in
that big dirty house with cracked wooden floors

in Hamilton, New York, and stuck my head
just over the quilts in my attic bed
to read your books against the cold, you kissed

(as I am kissing in blue telegrams),
found your love in atlases and road signs,
or virgin in your thought, impossible

to call her, you collected the shadows
slowly, rejoicing in the huge sorrow
of departure, and took hunger and ghosts

into the sleep you refused nightly. Shades
couldn't keep her blond stars out of your arms,
and you saved me with daybreak on each page

of your own isolation. I got up, darting
into the bathroom with the broken skis,
testing the midnight truth on the mirror

and outran a mouse back to your pages
where we each were holding our lover, not
asking, out of fear it might be untrue.

Then back to the galleries where you met
her soul speeding in an orange car, clear
of clouds, farther, farther into the doors

of the north where she was to be unknown,
a dwarf light on the maritime sky chart,
piercing you in the ecstasy of vast

loneliness. But you never failed me.
Gone, as if dead young, she gave her shadows
for you to form. You found her flesh tasting

of faith, and she brought you out of the great
anonymity, away from those who
now have no death to die in life, back from

the immense bonehead of those night persons
who create no love. I slept and kissed. My dream
gaslight against the moon illuminated

your lover, now mine. A page of words was
truth enough. In the morning I took you
to my desk where her kiss outlasted lightning.

China Poems 1976

Cave of the Beijing Man

Soon after dawn red dust is in the sky
and old men shadow box

or jog in shorts around the block. Shanghai cabs
are driving on their horns

in the great Plaza of Heavenly Peace.
The masses in blue trousers

hurry to work, we go west by the silk route . . .
mirrors float on the paddies,

fields stink of human fertilizer, and hills
of green ink are fragrant

with herbs and mist . . . the ancient cave
is empty. We climb down

and rub our fingers futilely on the wall
where the cranium was stuck.

The Beijing Man is gone. He may be in a
marine's footlocker or

at the bottom of the Pacific or in a
Japanese coffee shop.

His forty comrades of the cave have also
split. They stopped breathing

about half a million years ago . . . the masses
in blue trousers hurry to work

and dig up ancient coffins of an emperor
or greatly raise production

in a rubber shoe or paper factory. We have
been dying for a long time.

After Midnight in the Streets of Beijing

Red dust has fallen for the night
and I should sleep too, but I slip

downstairs, hop across the marble
grade where the chauffeurs hang out, and

suddenly in a city with
only a few eating places

open, the avenue of fans
is an empire of locust trees

where the moon with its cement face
glares on the few creatures moving

below: a tank truck watering
the tar, a lone sweeper, and me.

My feet have swollen from some dread
disease or from climbing the Long Wall

but I couldn't care less. I leap-
frog over a big steel trash can—

no one spots me—and am almost lost
in the great underground metro

where Beijing is to hide out when
the million Russian troops across

the border let the rockets fly.
I fly like a fire in a bamboo

forest, all alone in empty
China. How lucky I am here,

with all these ancient alleys of
jade where three emperors came from

their village to find the apples
of silk. I knock quietly at

a thin door in a dark patio,
walk in happy and disappear.

Snow

Summer collapses like a red flag
and I turn into now,
a snow mountain with no mountain inside. Just
dark bones needing a new shape.
I face it. Turn into nothing. And must go
to Central Asia to make a new self.
The cadre also judge and exile me to that countryside,
supposing it a punishment.
When I get there, the old paper house is remote.
I am a woodcutter in the mountains
and have a hut. I sing, cook yellow herbs,
and my Han and Dai friends laugh at me.
We drink beer under the moon and hear oil lamps
                    and panthers.

It is my last voyage.
And when death finally inks me out,
I lose nothing. That all fell far ago
like a red flag.
Only a pear tree that no one can hear is talkative.
Like geese fading over a river over a river,
every illusion is snow.

Eating Alone in a Cell in Changsha Attended by a Plump Waitress from Hunan Province

I hated to eat alone, and so loafed a while
                outside around the House of the Dead
or walked up and down the corridors, by small stores,
                where scissors and socks and cigarettes
were on sale, and by the Men's Room where soldiers
                trudged in and out buttoning their pants.
Finally I faced it and entered the cell. The food,
                delicious of course, was always hot,
and my friend who served me orange soda and rice
                came to talk and we wrote out words
for each other. But then she would disappear
                and I'd be alone for an hour, and no
Hunanese face, beaming, would come till I got up
                to go. I learned to fool her. I would
rise to leave, and my friend came in with hot towels
                for the last ceremony. I used
them, and sat down again to talk. She went along
                but worried about my impossible
tricks. I got her big, peasant, pepper eyes to laugh,
                and with every Chinese word I owned
I kept her there. Not again cut off in the House
                of the Dead! In China every hour
counts, is counted. Solitude has a deep bull-like

force, but I could scream like a pig
for distance and empty loss in my eating room.
              The screens guarded the sun. I made
this tablecloth, peopled with pork and jiaozi, a map
              with ten thousand friend and plum hills
when my friend and her human history slipped outside,
              leaving me bloated, hungry, alone.

Canton Hotel Room

You are shaving in the corner of the room.
Bolivia again where no one knows you.

We always meet where no one remembers.

You are giggling naked and plump in white undershorts
              you fiddle with,
and your face is white with the third lather.
I lie back on the bed, on the bamboo sheet.
A girl comes in.
You laugh very pleased and are interested in the girl.
I would like to have her too. But you follow her
              and disappear.
Have you gone again forever?

You are back in the room and I sit up.
This time I will force it out of you.
Father, you've got to level with me.
What did happen?
Remember, I got the call and they said you jumped,
              and I went to the funeral.
I even chose the coffin
though I would not look when the lid was opened.

How can you be here now? In this room,
And always the same age
in every continent where we find it safe to meet.
You've got to level. Where did you go
                        after the fall?
How did you come back?
Vaguely a thorn bush of light rises from a dark chasm
and you are climbing up the steep side of an Asian
                  mountain, secretly, tree by tree . . . .
You are here in front of the bed.

As you open your mouth the phone rings.
Your first words fly out like yellow birds,
                  sun from the gray volcano!
But Comrade Yeh asks in her four-toned voice:
"Willis, are you awake?
We must hurry or you will miss the morning rain
                  from Canton."

Mechanically I turn on the fan,
the smog stirs outside on the factory skyline
                  of Chinese dawn,
the night collapses in the corner of the room
and you are dead again.
I say: "Yes, Comrade Yeh, I am up!"

Wandering Loose in Shaoshan

Peasants come down from the tea hills
                  where Mao hid from his father,
and children play on dirt ridges between the rice
                  paddies of silver water.
I escaped too
and head up the peak with the Buddhist shrine

60

on top.
A great old man in serf black
is carting his pole and water pails, and tells me
                he is fine. Yet I am brooding
about the cork trees and my sneaky flight,
and study the water buffalo's nose floating just
                over the water.
The animal and I rest our heads
                from ideology
as the sun becomes the quarter moon.

A wind sways a generation of sleeping birds
                flying below. Yellow cranes sip
                the night,
and in a deserted hut I study loneness
                by an oil torch,
                and love in another room.
The mango bird is in the gold tree
                of passion
just behind me,
but the Buddha in the shrine turns the globe around:
                when I glance back
                desire is gone . . . .

As a flash of eternity dies in the wick
I wander down the mountain to my good comrades
                waiting tensely
for their friend who may be lost.

Stickball on 88th Street   1978

Marbles

During the marble season we control
89th Street. Cars edge by. Only
        cabs use their horns.
        Alfred is a big
winner. He's got cigar boxes loaded
with peewees and aggies which he
        keeps in a schoolbag
        like a banker. I
am sloppier and have never gone
into the business of setting boxes
        out in the gutter
        for guys to shoot
at the square holes. I hang
a few leather pouches from my
        belt and the rest
        are crunched in pockets
so I can hardly sit at school.
I make lots of noise when
        I run. The art
        of shooting from midway
in the street at a single,
between a double, or through a
        hole is not luck.
        It takes good eyes
and thought. Of course you have
to hit boxes that pay off.
        I'm a shooter, and
        do ok if the
street isn't warped, but I'm not
an acer. Some guys hit all
        the time or flip
        you for cards and
clean you out. We have trouble

when a car wants to park
          and the doorman makes
          us move. Then Alfred
and I sometimes go to his
house where we drop marbles on
          passing cars from the
          roof. We can hear
Jan Pierce rehearsing by holding an
ear against the elevator shaft door.
          I like to jump from
          the indoor balcony down
to the sofa, and don't really
know why it upsets Mrs. Freedman
          so much. I always
          like to jump or
climb. When I leave Alfred, I
go back to the street where
          it's getting dark. A
          big skinny red-haired kid
is walking by himself. And suddenly
I wrestle him to the ground —
          I don't know why
          I start it. We
roll on the sidewalk a while
and then I get back to
          the marbles where there
          are only a few
boxes still going. It's cold and
the Park wind rips through blue
          light and smashes me,
          gets through my knickers
as I head for the Drive.
I don't use the entrance but
          turn the wild corner
          and climb to my window.

The Boys Who Climb the Marble Squares
on the Soldiers and Sailors Monument

Last year one of them got
killed. He fell from the marble
        cylinder into the pocket
        between the columns and
onto the tar. Most of those
kids are colored. I got up
        twice to the eagle.
        It is just three
stories to the bird, easy climb,
but it took weeks to get
        myself to do it,
        and I stay there
all afternoon, enjoying my warm nest,
terrified to look down. The boys
        who climb the marble
        squares just hop into
my booth and shimmy to the
ledge under the squares. They always
        run around it first,
        shouting dirty words. Then
the real climb. The ones who
look poorest in their undershirts are
        the toughest. They crawl
        up, insects. Very few
make the rim circling round near
the ceiling. Then no place to
        go but to hang
        a while from it,
dangle as from a far wing,
hang all their toughness over the
        ocean of air that
        won't hold them up

Ice Picks on 93rd Street

I am wandering like a sailor
on the Drive. Eliot told me
                Life had an article
            on how babies are
born, with pictures of women.
I don't suppose I'll see *Life*,
                but oh it's great
            to think about them
slowly. Women. Between their legs is
what I see. Suddenly three ice picks
                are against my ribs.
            It's the Price gang.
Brothers. They've been to a reformatory,
I have a nickel but jam
                it into the lining
            and when they search
me they get nothing. But I'm
like stone, unbreathing, so scared I
                feel like a pickle
            with their spikes inside.
When the Price gang is gone
all those blond heads and pug
                noses seem alike. The
            Irish toughs from Amsterdam!
I don't hate them. I thought
they'd be worse. "Empty your pockets
                or we'll stick you."
            I didn't think they
would. But I can't walk there
for weeks, as if the brothers
                are always there, waiting
            to knife me for
cash. Eliot said the girls uptown let

you touch their hair or get
in their bed if
you have money. Now
I'm cocky. I've been held up
with ice picks against a dark wall.
Maybe like the sailors
I'll kiss a girl.

Stickball on 88th Street

I'm not much good at stickball
and the kids are tough. Somehow
it's my turn. In
comes the rubber ball
slowly in a dream like a
planet that won't spin. It comes
close, a blazing milky
rubber pea. I swing.
Bop! My childhood skids along windows,
dropping fair behind a manhole. I
race scared, ripping out
to second, miles away.
I must tag the lamp post first,
get by the toughs, not piss
in my pants or
bite my tongue. Why
didn't I dump the marbles when
I got up to bat? They
rattle in my knickers
pockets. Second is far
as Maiden Lane. If I slip
I'm out! No one's my friend
on this block, If
I make it, I'll

pass semaphore and learn to kip
on the highbar. The boys are
                screaming for me to
                run. For me! I
round second. Two kids are yelling
up the street, after the ball,
                as it bounces toward
                wild yellow taxis thumping
down West End. I fly home
through the mobs of black angels.
                Tonight I'll even snatch
                supper from the dog.
The ball floats home. I'm safely
standing on the side with guys
                shoving me. I'll never
                get to bat again.

Lucy Thibodeau

My first memory of life is
you holding me on steps outside
                a hospital where they
                snipped out my tonsils.
Maybe I am two. We are
already engaged and go steady till
                I am five. Overhead,
                a NY cement sky
more like a photo than a
memory. I am so in love
                with you! Mother is
                jealous and you won't
let her come near. When you
marry the doorman Jimmy and leave
                and have your own

child (who never learns
to walk), I feel bleak. All
I know for sure is how
                good when Jimmy dumps
                you (I am ten)
and we fix it for me
to come daily to your place
                for lunch between classes.
                I run up the
tenement stairs to the smell of
soup. I kiss a French beauty
                and we talk like
                old times. Now the
adventure will last for life (I
think) and never see you again.
                In the fall my
                sister writes that you
have aged, are thin, are spirited
as always. I think of you
                only a few times
                a year. You formed
me perhaps and time unformed the
work. When you kissed me, what
                did you think? Were
                mountains infinitely tall? Was
the day just one soup
of 10,000 splendid vermicelli soups
                for the elegant court
                of our futurity? Did
you know you would ever get
skinny and die? Other women I
                have loved disappeared too.
                They form you. You
touch them and go away. You
held me for five years, Lucy.

What luck to have
known you, a beauty,
and then you fled for 100
years into the snow to live
in poverty with your
sisters. We come, we
go. It is not different from
death. Thanks for coming to
the window each noon
to look for me
down the stairwell, for not fooling
yourself about how we had to
fail, about how good
we were, how like
insects, cities, and firmaments, we appear
and flare and fall apart. In
that Maine village with
your wheelchair son, I
am outside the house on the
Auburn hill, looking in, completely dumb.

A Bloody Saturday Night

I had been boxing for years.
Now at eleven, skinny but good
muscles, I am the
only one who dares
fight Lenny. Lenny is an animal,
my friend, but he demolishes anyone
who spars with him.
So I can't believe
that I'm really up to Lenny.
But my buddies do and I
am starting to think
I have a chance

of putting him away. That photo
at Old Orchard Beach still haunts
            me. There I am
            against a wall, my
legs twined to keep it in.
And the second picture with all
            my pants wet, still
            smiling. It is
the joke in our house. And
this pisher — who used to have
            to hang camp sheets out
            to sun dry in front
of anyone who cares to look
and laugh — is taking on Lenny
            in front of mobs
            of campers. I'm David
facing a monstrous Philistine in the
same hall where during morning service
            they told the story
            of the dancer between
two armies, more glorious than Pharaoh
in an ivory chariot. The bell
            brings us out. Lenny
            has lightning-quick mitts. We
dance around the huge ring, trading
jabs. I smash him in the
            bread-basket. The ref
            warns me. I tag
him behind the ear. He gets
his glove in my armpit, and
            we waddle like pros.
            I hear nothing. As
I move in I make an
old mistake: Lenny pops me under
            the chin just when
            my tongue is out.

A stream of blood jets eight
feet in a red arc from
        my mouth, and suddenly
        the ref saves Lenny
on the run, from a holocaust.
They take me from the hall
        to a nurse who
        stitches up my tongue.
It is dark. Though my career
fizzled, the sand by the lake
        and ping pong tables hold
        me up in glory.

The Building

Babe Ruth lives on the other
side of the court. His brother-in-law
        jumped from the 18th
        story into the handball
area where we play until tenants
get angry. I heard the thump
        when I was in
        bed. The Babe gave
me a baseball diploma. The same
Elevatorman, Joe, who slapped me for
        not being nice to
        Jerry (it wasn't true)
took me to the Babe's for
the photo that came out in
        The Mirror. Sunday afternoons
        we hear Father Coughlin
        and Hitler live, shrieking
on the radio. Everyone hates Hitler.
When there's a strike, new men

keep billy clubs by
the doors. I like
the scabs as much as Ruddy
and Joe outside to whom we
bring sandwiches. I heard
Ruddy got hit trying
to bust in. They almost broke
his head. It's funny for men
to ride me up
the elevator. I always
run downstairs. They slow me down
as I race for the outside
into the north pole
wind and the gully.
But often I spend the afternoon
in a corner of the elevator,
going up and down
in the tired coffin.
When no one else is riding,
they let me close the brass
gate. I do it
like a grown man.

Neil the Elevatorman

Neil's teeth are rotted, his hair
blond and stringy but his eyes
are weak sea blue
and kind. When his
car is not busy he lets
me ride up and down. At
times he comes to
the door to talk.
He is a vegetarian. We had

a maid named Meek Shyness who
                    belonged to Father Divine
                    but Neil's the first
vegetarian. He is the first intellectual
I meet (what they call him
                    in our house with a laugh).
        .   They are suspicious of
Neil, though they say he is
kind and probably harmless. He's poor,
                    lives alone and reads
                    all the time. I
am one of his real friends.
he tells me, and for me
                    he is very important.
                    The afternoon the Normandie
was burning, he took me up
to the roof and we stood
                    with crowds of people
                    watching the flames. It
was the first time so many
people from the building were together
                    talking easily. Neil gives
                    me books to read
and I take food from the icebox
for him. I am surprised and
                    happy that he has
                    different thoughts on everything.
I want to be like him,
to be poor, live in one
                    room, eat what I
                    will, and be alone
to think differently. He doesn't care
what they call him. I know
                    he's been let go
                    for talking to tenants.

Bessie

Cousin Bessie is a red. She
is our only political and poor
                relation. We all like
                Bessie and say she's
a good woman whatever she thinks.
She came from Russia with nothing
                but a pair of
                black galoshes. Dad likes
to take her on when she
comes for Thursday supper (Leah's off)
                and always gets cold
                meals, maybe a pineapple
upside-down cake, if any is left.
We sit down to borscht, horseradish
                and gefilte fish. Bessie
                dumped her husband Max
who fought with the Abraham Lincoln
and lost a finger. "How's Max?"
                I ask her one
                night. "That bum?" she
answers. Max studied watchmaking but refused
to eat on anything but newspapers.
                Bessie used to live
                in a Bronx basement
in which the icebox leaked, but
she's downtown now and her feet
                don't hurt so much
                from walking. Bess brims
with love. She loves Stalin and really cares
for workers and all poor people.
                Her kisses are famous:
                huge, noisy and slubbery,
and she's so kind and concerned.

She always asks first about me,
                Billy. I go to
                see her and we
talk politics—my first lessons—but
she warns me not to repeat
                all this to my
                parents. She's always worked,
worked. Recently she took a few trips
and came back hatted and smiling.
                We are her only
                relations. Her age is
a mystery and joke at home.
She hasn't called so we go
                downtown. Bessie's on the
                floor, a week dead.

Blondie

Mother is calm like our Chinese
rug—and firm like the Tree
                of Life a painter
                put in the wool.
Her eyes are Maine forest green.
She is real as a painting
                and just as constant.
                Dad calls her Blondie
and she's unreal as an angel
because she keeps mountains of heaven
                inside her, which I
                know nothing of, and
only Sunday morning when I invade
Mom and Dad's room and bounce
                on their bed do
                I rouse her to

shoo me off like a monkey
out of India. But she never
                screams or weeps or
                bellyaches. I listen to
the Green Hornet or read funnies
till supper when she can't get
                me to eat onions.
                She doesn't talk easily
but her word is a temple.
She is good, and never gives
                me hell, yet her
                word is there, unsaid
and strong. It's strange to be
so strong and soft at once:
                a woman. She is
                a mystery to me
like women or God or solid
geometry which I'll know one day
                in high school. She
                loves me I know
because of what I overhear her
say to Blanche or Sadie or
                other friends. Mother is
                clear and deep like
a Chinese print with mist, and
I love her like some cloud
                beyond quiet bamboo mountains
                (far inside the frame).

Skating

As a scout I'm a loser
and slob. I make First Class
            but how? In the
            New Jersey forest where
we bivouac, I cook a pie
by filling pre-made dough with canned
            stewed tomatoes. I lay
            the leaky mess in
an outdoor fire with potatoes, and
when it burns black, I take
            it to the scoutmaster.
            "You eat, you pass."
So I pass cooking. I also
win an axe for selling raffles,
            but my uniform never
            fits. I'd rather skate
than march. When spring gets rid
of the ice, the boys start
            hockey. I'm not good
            enough for the team
and skate off, gliding lengths
from the street to street. I've gone all
            the way to Harlem
            and the East Side.
No place lies beyond my rollers.
I dance backwards and take leaps
            like an artist. And
            I like to go
alone. I find my skinny body
as it flies through the wind.
            On Sunday when I
            gaze out the window
at the warships sailoring the

river, and my head is bursting
in this empty house,
I take my skates
to the Drive. I put them
on as an actor puts on
paint. Then I skirt
the flocks of families and pigeons;
race from tier to tier of
marble sky, and roll across
stone benches in exultation!

Overnight Train

We go to camp by Pullman
from Grand Central Station. 50 groups
leave the madhouse
Sunday. I try to
nap in the luggage hammock, then
go constantly up and down from
my berth into
the washroom, which stinks
of steam and smoke, whose cold
and hot faucets are curved like
the dining car's oversize
spoons. Amid the clacking
metals, the black porter is bent
asleep. Back in the starched sheets
and tight tan blanket,
I hear the wheels
all night, the squeaking, the ponderous
thumping and whizz. As we speed
I gaze eagerly at
the darkness. I am
the night. The black firmament starts

on my sheet and goes outward
            to planets on the
            ceiling 500 miles away.
I draw open the heavy curtain
and watch cows looking at me,
            see white clapboard sheds
            as upright as gravestones.
My eye is huge and tingles,
holding all those outdoor ghosts and
            half moon. Finally, sleep
            lies on me. I
watch it come, control it like
the narrow berth-lamp over the window.
            Each time I turn
            the bulb on, all
becomes a small cell with fire.
I got into sleep, deep into
            a time absolutely still
            except for the wheels
alertly blazing North. When tiny morning
tapes the fields with amazing sun,
            I hear cocks, bells.
            The cows are still
giving the yellow meadows a haircut.
I shimmy down and rock toward breakfast.

The Woods

There is a trail around the lake
in the woods that goes up
            to a mountain. We
            hike in the morning.
Hal picks up wintergreen and chews
the leaf. I have a canteen

and a Bowie knife.
We are looking for
the secret meadow where the blueberries
are already out. I fall behind
(I always do, even
later on the Great
Wall) and get lost. "We'll meet
on the mountain" someone yells. In
northern Maine the air
is knife blade cool
in July, Caesar's month, and pines
don't know ice from summer. But
I come on an
orchard with barbed wire
and poison ivy on the rails.
Abandoned. The apples are pieces of
red fire and taste
like fire water. I
have to shit. I'll catch up.
Am worried about the leaves mixed
with dirt I have
to use. Voices fade.
Under an apple tree is a perfect
stick for whittling a walking cane.
I sit in the
sun and pare bark
from the cedar branch. It's nice
in the sun, lying down. Sun
floats up there, a
ship, and directly under
it is me. I close my
eyes and it is violet under
the lids, a sea
almost. For a few
hours I sleep. Then get up

and finish the cane. When I
　　　　　get to the mountain,
　　　　　no one's there, but
I collect blueberries, all I can
cart back. The sun is gone
　　　　　as I turn back.
　　　　　I bound quickly through
the woods, stumbling against a birch,
squashing the berries in my pocket.
　　　　　　Some hours after midnight
　　　　　　I find my tent.

The Couch

When Aunt Jane or someone else
stays over, I sleep by myself
　　　　　(the guest's with Mother)
　　　　　on the living room couch.
The big room has a blue
Persian rug, a Bubble boy done in
　　　　　1900 by Mrs. Adams
　　　　　our neighbor in Maine,
and fake marble antiques from France
of the 17th century done in
　　　　　1910. When I perform
　　　　　acrobatics on the rug
I stop and look at the
Bubble Boy looking at me. His hair
　　　　　is angel gold. He
　　　　　never finishes the pipe.
I think he's me. Tonight I stay up.
No one tells me about my
　　　　　body except to eat
　　　　　quickly, although I'm deeply

curious. In the bathtub my dong
floats and I steer it through
                    sponges and soap foam
                    until the last water
drains out and its face lies
on the cold porcelain. Now I'm
                    on my back. NY
                    stars and the lights
from Central Park come in through
the Venetian blinds, in the dark
                    living room. I am playing
                    acrobatics with my dong,
playing pinochle quickly. It's a Jack
of Spades looking for a Queen
                    of Hearts. I seize
                    and hurt it! It's
climbing up away from me when
it shudders and shoots out something
                    not piss, the sweetest
                    pain on the planet.
It drains me and the fury
suddenly stops. I think I've leaked
                    or broken a piece
                    of my body. I'm
alarmed and happy. Maybe it's ok.
I say nothing. Late next evening
                    I can hardly wait
                    till the next room
is silent. The Bubble Boy is dark
and only those bits of light
                    from the city sky
                    shine over the couch
where I try out the secret
game again. With slow fury I
                    play the same Jack

until I get lost
eagerly in a flooding white sea.
It comes! It goes out almost
        as strong. The Queen.
        I'm in 100 rooms.

Women

Eliot says babies come out of
a woman's stomach through
        her legs. He tells
        me so one afternoon
as we walk by the river
at nightfall. I've never seen where
        a girl pisses from
        and think no one
has. If I were a girl
for a few days, I'd look
        with a mirror and
        find out every secret.
I don't know any girls. They
play jacks and hopscotch, prance around
        on the sidewalk while
        we're in the street.
About five years ago when I
was six—so long ago it's
        hazy—I saw, or
        almost saw, two girls
behind some rocks in the park
pull off their panties on purpose.
        They were kids, too,
        jumping up and down
and yelling. I knew two women
for a short time. Last year

I walked Sarah Whitehall
home, and even went
up to her apartment and met
her mother. I liked her. It was
odd and fun walking
on the sidewalk with a girl. We
talked about Joe Louis who had
just put Max Schmeling
in the hospital. Sarah
asked me to a party where they
would play spin-the-bottle, post office, and
strip poker. I went
but she'd moved away
and all we did was dunk
for apples and play blind-man's-bluff.
Varda Karni is different,
She's dark. Her hair
is beautiful. Her parents take her
to many cities in the Middle
East. I'm good at
school and tell her
what I know about astronomy and
art. I have a crush. She
seems to fly in
from far Fifth Avenue
and Ethical Culture. She has swept
through the Museum of Natural History
and smiles at me.
I don't know what
she thinks. A mystery. I give
her a copy of Homer's *Odyssey*
and one day at
the door she comes
to bring a big letter and quickly
goes. I take it to the

blue living room, open two
sheets of white paper
inside each other, and a third
sheet carefully folded to a small
square. It is blank
inside. Not a word,
not even Varda. Eliot says he
knows a lot more about women,
as we slog home,
and one day will tell.

Street People

Old people sit on benches next
to the subway on upper Broadway
or along the Drive.
At times they talk,
often they put their hands flat
on the arm-rests and gaze for
hours. They seem to
be thinking but their bodies are
not moving. Some are what are
called refugees. Near Grant's
Tomb with its lively
stone horse, there's always one old
lady whose face is shaped like
a Singer sewing machine,
whose hair is white
grass, who uses her cane to
knock nuts across the octagonal paving
stones on which both
squirrels and pigeons circle
her. On a side street I see
a man in sandwich boards advertising

sneakers pull his penis
out and leak next
to the gutter. He has white
stubble on his cheek, fat shoes
and looks blank when
I look at him.
I am curiously ashamed. His eyes
scan the buildings, then look down
as he clears his
nose. Up by Joan
of Arc, an old guy, round
as a tomato, in a narrow
store sells pastrami sandwiches
to us between classes
at 4¢ apiece. "Who next,
who next," he shouts. I hardly
recall my mother's mother
and father. She outlived
him, though her hands were shaking
and we couldn't make the slightest
noise. When the ambulance
came last night, its
white body sucked in a stretcher
and the machine sped off. The
doorman said the super's
girl died of polio.
I wonder what I'd do if
swimming across Lake Beebee my arms
tired, if I took
in sky water, drowned
and faded to the bottom and became
the whole world in my head
and couldn't get back
in time for classes.

Dreaming

I search the sky. The window
facing the Hudson and Jersey coast
        is my Saracen tower
        from where I spot
bonfires of Crusaders, or blue cops
clubbing the park trees methodically as
        they walk their beat.
        At twilight I study
God whom I've been making up
since I remember. He is not
        like my father, who
        is good. God is
what they say Father is: an
angry, crazy man. So I've abolished
        God, because I want
        my Dad. I see
a white horse at night over
an iceland with hungry leopard seals.
        Suddenly the new moon
        is frozen like a dancer.

The Family

Sometimes I go down to Wall Street
and the office on Maiden Lane.
        We come up out
        of the subway like
birds soaring out of a sewer.
Goldsmiths, Pildes! These stores are cities
        with everything man invented
        in crystal and steel
like Brahms played by Mrs. Friedburg

my teacher from Germany. Dad is
                    walking with me. NY
                    spring sun makes us
feel happy. Suddenly Dad takes off
his felt hat with a curse.
                    A pigeon shat on
                    its light gray dome.
Till then I didn't know birds
could do that to people. Before
                    we go into Schrafts,
                    I race ahead to
a lamp post and climb up. He
doesn't mind. I remember they found
                    a light fedora on
                    the roof when he
jumped into the spring sky. Smell
of mint and blueberry twinges in
                    the air. We're eating
                    cheese pie. The waitresses
are fat and creamy like the
pie. Up in the office Dad
                    lends cash to a
                    black Jewish sailor who
missed his ship. Mom, Dad, and
I subway home with three newspapers.
                    Tired. Dad alertly reads
                    The World Telegram. Tonight
we'll all hear *Information Please.* By
morning when I hear Father screaming
                    "You God damn bitch,
                    you. You God damn
bitch, you," he is furious and
gets out the door. Mother and
                    I go back into
                    the rooms. As when

the bird shat on the light
gray dome of Dad's new hat,
        I'm surprised. I feel
        thin and now alone.

The Doorman Lets My Father
Come Upstairs Unseen
Through a Side Entrance

At twilight the doorman and I
go around the corner to a
        door I never saw
        that lets my father
in directly to the back stairs.
The cars on the Drive are
        sedate, carrying authority from
        downtown, uptown. We are
New Yorkers and don't own one.
Where is my father coming from?
        A place they have
        cars? From the city?
It's the first time he's back,
and no reason for neighbors, who
        are strangers, to know.
        He is not afraid
but is not beaming. It's funny
to sneak him in like Jews
        out of a ghetto
        to get food, as
if he were guilty for being
my mother's husband. He is happy
        we make it in,
        as if we went
out on the road and sold

a diamond. I'm up again when
               he goes down white
               iron back steps, by
the boiler room, and up to the
wood-and-brass side door. There are only one
               or two solitary cars
               rolling outside. It is
almost twilight. I kiss my father
before we open the door. He
               steps unshaven into half
               light. Maybe in a
week he'll call from out there,
from miles into the light, and
               we'll meet at the
               zoo or down below.

Selling

Father has lost everything: the business,
his wife and children, his wild
               confidence. I'm with him
               for a long summer at
the Greystone Hotel. I have to
study Latin and when we're not
               talking or out selling,
               I follow Julius Caesar
into Gallia and that farthest outpost
where the hairy Britons live. Our
               room faces Broadway, but
               we're high enough not
to hear the noise. The Greystone
has known better days. We say
               we don't care. It's
               good to be together.

He shows me how to shave
and I practice carefully, imitating his
                stroke and the way
                he uses his fingers.
He has nothing left from the
company but three valises: mainly straps,
                eight fancy gold watches
                in modern shapes, some
semiprecious stones and a few
small diamonds. We figure about $500.
                Enough to live through
                the summer. And then?
What we sell we share for
rent and food. I am thrilled
                because I am with
                Dad. He's showing me
things, and we often chat through
the night, from bed to bed,
                with the deepest confidence.
                I adore him, and
he always tells me I'm his
one love. But he is pained
                and depressed, though he says
                with me he's not.
We take the IRT to Wall
Street and systematically make the rounds
                of each jewelry store.
                Some of the owners,
old clients, recognize Father. He gets
furious, embarrassed, or glad according to
                what they say. We
                lay the valises with
straps on the counter and Dad
begins to sell. I too add
                key information about soft

Swiss leather. If we
sell 2 gold watches and 100
watchstraps, we can make it through
                a week of diners
                and the Greystone. If
we have a good day we celebrate
at Starkers or some better place.
                Dad shows me how
                to read a newspaper
in the subway, folding it correctly.
What will we do when it's
                all gone? Yet Father
                trades a few stones
and buys a diamond with all
he's got left. He sells it
                a few days later,
                doubling our cash. Now
he brings out the stones first.
On Sundays we boat or go
                out to a beach
                or watch the seals.
He's thinking of leaving the city.
We make all kinds of plans
                at night. I see
                him shaving, his face
lathered and sparkling. One late afternoon
we are strolling up Broadway. I'd been
                studying Latin words for
                hours. The top papers
on the stand read: GERMANS INVADE
POLAND! WORLD WAR! Father's going west
                and I must soon
                separate again from him
when we have finally found ways
to be free, to keep all

riches in a tiny
velvet cloth, and laugh.
One day in China I dream
of Father coming into the room.
He's shaving. He's come
back to talk again.

The Call

I am with you in NY
at a hotel. You're in bad
shape. Just a year
ago in Colorado we
all walked with the wirehair bouncing
on the sidewalk. You put in
a line direct to
Denver and were to
civilize the world with silver goblets.
You've moved too quickly again. We
talk about it through
the night. You've dropped
so low I seem to be
your father now. I speak firmly,
telling you to resist.
Why do I speak
this way? Something prods me. Perhaps
that's what you need. But we
do talk well. You
know as always I
love you. And I know what
I am to you. I have
to go back to
Maine to finish up
the term. I don't like to

leave you. Now I'm the only
        one of us you
        see. We say goodbye
and I promise to see you
soon. Back at school, I hope
        you will pull money
        out of the sky,
you will somehow fight and feel
better. It's finals here and I'm
        cramming. My roommate Bernie
        from Austria tells me
not to worry so much. But
he's pre-med, works like hell too.
        The phone rings. Dad.
        "Can you come down
right away to NY?" "You must
be crazy," I say, "This is
        exam week. I'll mess
        up the whole term."
I am angry. I am surprised
that I'm impatient, but something prods
        me. "Please come." "Dad,
        I can't. Please wait
till I get through finals. Are
you ok?" We talk some, but
        I can't remember words.
        He's in bad shape.
I shout at his sadness which
is piercing me. "I'll see you
        soon," I say. Click.
        The week is a blur
but I'm on the golf course
with Roberto and Hans from Mexico,
        first time I've played.
        We come back late,

a bit slaphappy after the grind.
"Someone's been trying to reach you
            all afternoon." I call
            back. My Dad's assistant
in Colorado. "Your father left NY
for Mexico. Then he flew here.
            He jumped around noon
            from the top of
this building. Are you coming
to the funeral?" I leave for
            NY. No one else
            is going out West
except a business friend Jack who
is loyal although stuck with debts.
            They tell me he
            folded his topcoat neatly
and put his felt hat alongside
before he swan dived and forgot to
            float back up through
            the warm May air.
There are some silver goblets left
I take with me. I cannot look
            at his face. I
            don't want to remember
anything but my father live. The
air has a mountain clarity. It
            is beautiful there. I
            will not be alive
the same way again without him.
I can't take that untaken trip
            to NY. He is
            with me even now.

Overheard   1979

Overheard

1

I want to live
I want to die
love is want to
live no love is
death I want I
am alone I am
I want to love

2

thirst the body
needs water the
heart needs blood my
heart is a well
it wants more blood
to live is to
thirst for water

3

a child is a
sleeping good poem
the sun is in
the sleeping eyes
of a child all
good things in the
sun fill a child

4

my life who cares?
I care yet want
a you not me
to care the dog
sleeps all the day
I live all life
and care and you?

5

time is a drug
it is always
now yet it kills
I can almost
not stand time it
is pain the sin
of nature death

6

all day I think
just me here here
thinking now I
sleep and still dream
it means I am
the blue hill is
I want to stay

7

I hate my self
with some love and
guilt a hot day
falls on my hair
if I can I
will love your face
body and mind

8

I must die and
not know why life
fell on me it
is a cheap black
trick it makes me
try to outsmart
the dark dark dark

9

I was weak but
so was a child
I did not know
and waited time
is hitting me
they say I look
young time is strong

10

I must if a
spoon can drink all
the yellow sun
I must not wait
for light to come
the dark is deep
and full of sun

11

when I don't sleep
I gulp a pill
when I don't think
I am just gone
when I dug holes
in Mexico
there was hope hope

12

I don't know when
I lie I mean
the deep secret
untruth I go
about in a
sane face which
means I am mad

13

if you were more
I would be glad
bliss would be here
if you not me
or truthfully
we were more the
hill O the hill!

14

on life it is
bitter one life
I am not the first
but some had God
if I were full
I could die but
then I should live

15

please yet who are
you? before when
I ask please say
a word please you
must understand
in the dumb mind
a word is hope

16

I lost my tongue
one year and found
the hollow space
which almost made
me free of me
with no flesh I
was wholly lost

17
when my back broke
the doctor came
like stars to a
sailor a sweet
wind the bed broke
and only a
strong broom was good

18
coffee is my pot
it floats the big
expanding dome
the sides fly out
breakfast slips fast
like a dogwood
far stretching far

19
the six selves of
me slip over
each other and
I am so dry
with sneaky nights
the peace of death
is almost good

20
you are like me
that is one good
one good bit of
life if you are
poor like me we
are two we are
a lonely mass

21
how can no one
know but the face
of easy group
doctrine? how can
no you I have
a clue why we
are? no one know?

22
some give up but
most never come
to the question
I am tortured
like an old Jew
in a camp he
knows O please
wait

23
no I can wait
and if death strikes
I won't believe
it I always
said yes there will
come a fire peace
a word a love

24
I am not bored
but dull at times
and hot and like
a child who can't
wait for a toy
bored like a frog
hopping a beast

25

when the beast rang
the monastery
big bell I jumped
and ate black bread
and read two nights
and sang sang poor
poor O but loud!

26

the polka dots
fell like a dog
when a steak sits
in its pan my
robe held in a
nude body she
sailed on a room

27

three candles sat
and laughed at me
my toes froze heart
choked in the pipes
the city was bad
in every street
I ran I ran!

28

alone but a
fly keeps the jazz
band loud and loud
it hits a bulb
I smash my eyes
in filaments
fly you are bright

29

slowly I learn
about screws paint
typing yet dawn
bangs in on deaf
sleeping ears one
day I may wake
am I a fool?

30

I know pain it
comes making me
more alone more
then it is hard
not to sleep not
to sleep and sleep
a weak bad bed

31

spring is no one
can say no a
woman is like
a spring lovely
sometimes if a
beautiful thing
is yes it is

32

I sank lay on
silver paper
toy wrecked when
my child woke up
to kiss me what
shame joy I lay
high on a flag

33

the man who was
in this head was
not in one place
I don't know the
exact spot can't
find him I talk
look am I? where?

34

the tongue is part
of the head but
it goes like a
self-winding watch
I watch it flap
back with its own
words I am far!

35

food goes inside
oxygen comes in
I drive a car
the body works
it works wrong the
dark is so dark
food but no light

36

I trace it may-
be a worm birds
now break the dawn
dawn is outside
O birds the quiet
of your loud cry
miracles almost

37

the birds are mad
weep weep weep no
they are birds dawn
my knees are tight
if the pen dries
I can sleep no
the birds are mad

38

I would pay but
how my soul talks
but so what no
god makes it a
good buy before
I leave maybe
the soul will burn

39

I am poor how
can you or
be I fully glad
a second may
be enough one
kiss light fire head
we are still poor

40

yes it is good
to breathe and how
bad because I
know I will stop
can any light be
strong enough to
help for the dark?

41
light is in hell
but just as strong
as concrete love
is it is just
as clear as day
love asleep
in the next room

42
the word is deep
it makes me sweat
daydream stay up
all night drink hot
milk bouillon pills
is there I'm not
mad but deep close

43
is it worth it?
I can choose it
choose to shoot me
with breath I see
a face and know
good eyes I can't
choose we are here

44
my tricks I play
because I can't
give up death draws
me it is strong
my tricks save the
sky a horse white
as salt shakes me

45
it this town in
this life I made
my bed if I
scream it is in
this room honey lands
are there I'm here
with a scream now

46
if I don't stop if
I don't dream if
light is not my
harbor if I
won't pick up the
hammer and club
my brain I stop

47
a sweet woman
is she's not fake
her breasts and groin
are sweet she is
on earth she loves
me and I her
she is I hope

48
the sun is so
deeply good sun
is so good and
day is now I
walk I fear but
O I know day
the sun I love

49
I feel your flesh
warm and funny
as a herring
you ride a bike
I ski slam the
door I drink you
your flesh is warm

50
light is in hell
and where dark is
water of pupils
you are light where
I am not I
wait for you who
are enough light

Snow Salmon Reached the Andes Lake 1980

Resolution

Summer near the cows and taste of blue thorns
with my closest friend (who died that fall).

We talk on two big glacial rocks
                under tasty sun
on our hill high like a grassy moon
over Brandon's white steeples and Mr Ketcham's barn.

I say I will change my life.
No, Larry says, it is not too late.
Birds scream. O but the day is deep with hope.

I don't fear joy but wait too long,
and when the night blows up slowly like an exploding
                bull
it is clear as pain

and I have changed my life.

Winter in this wholly dark bedroom
where I put my glasses on and waddle like a fool
graying
in the day around the chair clogged with dirty shirts
                for a watch that bounced on the floor.
It has the time.

I resolve there will be time
I do resolve
as on a summer New England rock
when Mr Ketcham's screaming children in the valley
                seemed like many birds.

This is not the time for truth.

Winds on the Tableland

You surprised me. I was sleeping on a bag of sand
                under poplar trees along the Duero River.
I had wandered on the tableland for three years
and never spoke to the peasants in the taverns
or smoked with the February winds
                inhabiting my sleeves.

Then you were there.
The reddish walls of the ancient city were not shocked.
The sandtrees and magnolias gave no sign
                to the winter moon.
The merchant threw out the delinquent mother
                and her bony children
while the planet rolled about its pin
                as on an ordinary day.

You came. Surprised the air and painted mountains
                with windy dictionary stars.
The massive news was a secret I smoked each night
                in my room
before the ordinary sun struck the tableland.

Dumb

I was angry
and foolish
and stone gray. Dumb as pain.
The clock in the church tower
cleared its lungs
and sang out.
Outside of town I forgot
and saw a yellow deer
spring calmly
through the grass.

Herons

In the morning
the rain and straw sun sat on the jungle meadows
                and chozas
and swamps where the bulls were belly deep in water.
Vultures sat like black teeth in all the plane trees,
waiting for a garbage truck to get hauled
                out of the mud.
In the swamp grass around the bulls
and near the naked asses of the dirty children
                of paradise
were the snow herons of peace.

With A Rhino by the River
for L.L.

After trekking a few weeks near Annapurna
                under the ice sun,
I bussed south down to the open jungle
and rented an elephant who munched a small palm tree
as we trudged through villages to the river.
A rhinocerous is torpid
yet when I concealed myself, uncautiously
behind a banyan tree,
                foolishly down wind,
the rhino signaled he wasn't envious of my elephant
or my little form in the dawn.
We gazed at each other for thirty minutes.
His eyes were cups of green water with genesis singing
                at the bottom.
Neither of us worried.
I wouldn't scoop his enormous weight and armor
                with a bullet.

115

He didn't care that I could read, and he preferred grass
    to my raw flesh.
I didn't covet his tusk sticking into heaven
even as a Chinese aphrodisiac.

A decade later I ponder on the great myopic beast
looking up from the river herbs to glare at me.
He is still the brown knight with elaborate plates of
    Asian armor hanging
beautiful under a root-tasty jungle breeze.
I wanted him for the adventure of the soul,
for a poem about a rhino charging and goring
                 an outsider.
He wanted nothing
and let me stand with him by the river.

Dream

Maybe these poems (which are half my life)
and my life too are not worth more
than guano or Pedro Domeq or a few drachma
    or a ton of phosphate. If so,
I would be pleased to leave now
for I am no son of the Buddha
or even of Jesus who came of my dark blood.
I am more a lobster in its pond.
Yet I stay a child with a sly dream
    of waking up,
unafraid of time, released, an orphan free.

Rooftop

for my father, d.,1946

You jumped so long ago
now it seems you were
never really here. I know
you were and remember
vaguely. If you could
fly back up to the ledge
and show up today
as you were, we would go
again out to the desert
or south of green Oaxaca
go on double dates.
We discovered what a window
was the afternoon we chased
bats out of our jungle room;
and if I also live close to
the roof, we share a secret
of the good cells on fire
in our black lungs. One night
I failed you. I said no
I could not come. The phone
clicked. You sailed so long
ago out of this world
yet I can't find where
to put that love: the pear
sapling I let wither or
the avocado tree you tore
out of yourself and me.
Our love lay folded neatly
with your coat and felt hat
found on the rooftop
on the day you swan dived
and forgot to sail back up
in the high open sunny air.

Patmos

The dream ends here. Beyond these solitary whales
        and seven stars
we wake. Here is peace. It is not ours.
By steamer we came to the cave of the Revelation
        where a boy is blowing bubble gum
        in the yellow air by the candles.
Is this the end? We lose and we begin, and climb
        nervously. Wind is wild noise.
Sun bakes the white crenelation on the hilltop monastery.
The heavens open and a white horse steps
        on mountains in the water.
Can we see? The daystars fall like figs
        cast down by the windmill gale.
The sea is glass mingled with fire.
Fire in us who love. We lose. We wake.
        On the wharf an octopus, in
        each tentacle a horse of salt
        shining like the seven stars.
The dream ends here. Fire in us who lose.
        In the dark cave we see.

Pension

On the third floor I live near a butler
        and carpenter who play cards
        each long evening in the kitchen
where they chew onions and gossip and leave
        pastry in the sink.
I care for them but they are weak wine
        left in the glass overnight.
Now I must burn our white rooms, clean the grease
        and cinders from the oven,

hold my breath a while
or gossip with the carpenter about the slum lord
and the priest.

But you and I in our dry beds
are luckier than the butler and his friend.
In our chaos, in our oven, in our birthday love
shot down like an outlaw prince,
I find my way in my head
to find my way to your room by the basso trains
and Mennonite barn,
and talk to you and comb your hair.

Wild Iris

In the small scholarly room
where we lived freely between books and lions
on a mountain of light,
the window over our bed would not shut
and a winter moon froze on us.
We lay close and kept warm under a Finnish drape.
When you got up to pee or wash
your soft return was a fawn in the iris
of a wild brook.
We were distinguished and perfect.

When you typed and typed through the dawn
and I the scholar of one candle
wrote and dozed,
we meandered freely like the goats in the sun
in the broken marble reading rooms
of Asian Pergamon
Our room froze. You typed. I hugged you,
made you tea and we kept warm.

Chapel

Midnight and observation jeeps parked by the Acheron
       and the unexplored temple
       and prison at Oropos with the composer.
We hear fever in our lungs
and climb carefully on blue mountains
       on the blue ledge over the bay of Euboia
to Saint Peter's small chapel
where we talk and love all night,
a night of milk
and fresh oranges you bring when we are tired.
Our white bird is no dream as it rains
       through the tender dark.
The secret police are sleeping in the room
       beside the royalist officers who failed.
Ferry boats begin to cross the grape morning bay.
You ask my name. It's dawn.

Half Moon

Among the hundred cypress trees I walked
       looking for my feet.

Over the marble mountain of Pendeli
       came the ship of light,

over shaved heads of tubercular children
       sleeping near the cats.

The half moon glazed like a butcher's lamp bulb,
       its dark half was my wonder.

I climbed in its black coffin. There I asked
       for more time near its light.

Cello

Tonight I took the cross and a coke bottle
              and heaved them in the sea
and had to dance very late alone in my room
where the two oil lamps laughed dryly.
Maybe I am learning how to act.

Your face was luminous and happy when you
              surprised me at the door;
you sat on your nightgown and we embraced.
All night the cello played outside and wandered
              on the red rooftops in the Sporades.
By dawn we were so fragile. We were alone
              and danced,
then dressed slowly by the fire of the owls.
Outside, the crane's wing shone in the rose
              of the early sun.
Your face was gone and shone.

Village

Three hawks hang under the harvest moon.
I walk alone at the edge of this ski
              village and worry,
for you who sleep in my ear on the linen hills
are a week away in your house on the rub-a-dub
              mountain.
Is the lamp all night again on fire
              at your smoky desk?

You took me to a high meadow of wind and brown-eyed
              susans,
              time blew among the yellow caraway,

time filled our sweet science
where a snow salmon reached the Andes lake.
We hiked up to the blue city of big stones,
   lay on stone pastures of the evening,
   lazily threw onions at the Inca stars
and laughed at Roman candles. Disappeared.

Three hawks hang over this village where the lamps
   are out. Cold as this slow hour
the peaks are icebergs near the moon.

Hunting

It is fall
and the Kikuyus are hunting as usual
   on the snow leopard plateaus.
Our captain America finds an oriental solution
   at Songmy
while at home the season is open for death.
Farmers and barbers enter the forest
   of brake and partridge and swamps,
creep like red ants up the Green Mountains,
raise their great phallus to their shoulders
   and pump fire
at the deer of love.

In high Kenya there is fresh snow
while six bulls die in the afternoon in the ring
   of the cheering city of Baeza.

Lions

Even in crazy gloom in the crater of fools
        I lie and daydream
of being that huge torso of Apollo lying cracked
        and serene on the beach
near the palm tree near the gold bridge
        from the ship called Parabola.
I lie
        for I see us
hand in hand along the sea urchin shore
        near the plaza of heat and fig trees.

We walk to the torso to the row of canine lions,
        archaic stone pitted with sun,
gazing alive like us at the sea way out.

Way out.
It is a yellow boat. It came and now is lost
        in haze
beyond the Theologian's cave and summit castle
        of monks;
beyond the high chalk village and nothing.
Revelation in the haze.
Through our common cloud of unknowing
        we love and grope
toward to a bit of snow we cannot see.

Travel

An hour before the dawn
I came with a red grip from the north.
In your gown you opened the winter door
        and in half belief we slept
        in half dream our bodies talked

tenderly and with lightning in our thighs
            we soared were fed.
Dawn came deeply in our flesh
and everywhere was dawn, dawn, dawn! The axe
            of time was gone. Rainbow
            of night salmon and sun.
We were fragile and joyful and huge.
            Rainbow.
            We went south
and spoke courteously with Indians and climbed
            together over ancient stones.

Morning of Herbs

I took your hand. In it were the fields
of thyme and the camomile we picked.
How many mornings of herbs were there?
Enough for two lives? After midnight we drove
in falling snow. Streets grew soft. Snow hid
            the Christmas fire
and the paper farmhouse in us that was to burn.
From the seaport we followed an orange butterfly
into a warm apple grove.
I put a cardboard bird in your arms. It was
            out last day
and so we briefly died on the fragrant meadow.

Five A.M. in Beijing   1987

Five A.M. in Beijing

Awake in Beijing darkness as a dream of thighs
           rips me out of sleep.
Outside the window in the carbon gas gloom
I hear the morning song of a gargling spitter
        in the brick alley,
           turning up like a baritone.
The city is wrestling with its throat
and searches deep in its lungs for yellow pearls.
Near daybreak another spitter warbles
before casting his puddle in our ears.
Then air comes alive with screaky sparrows,
someone is whistling, and the myna bird moon
flies slowly out of the night.

The stroller whistles a melody in the alley in five notes
as once on Skyros from a predawn bed
I heard drunk Greek friends chanting all the way
across the pine winter island.
Another sick terrible cough. The whistling persists,
military and ancient. Lying on my back
on an orange Turkestan rug,
again I hear the call outside.
I am ridiculous but hot and waiting
        for song and ascension
as first rays ignite with December's foul smoke,
as breakfast hunger jostles my loose pajamas,
as time—which is our dream the mechanical spy
        into the spirit—
pushes into gray factories growing in the dusk
and performs its second waiting.

Water Whitman

In fairly good health, fifty-six years old, a child
              of oriental adventure,
I ask you to look for me.
I am the stranger I cannot find.
If you want me, read me under these words.
They prove my grounds for extreme pessimism:
their banality, low soul, their rambling effort to sing
              myself
in their alphabet utterly deprived of grace.

But I don't accept my death. The notion sickens me,
especially in half sleep
when blank, in terror, I wake as a fetal ball.
I don't accept my age and work to cover it
with each shampoo, striped shirt, each dawn jog
outside the gates around the Youyi Binguan
and brood, less than before, about an insipid life.

I wait for everything, good poems, for you to think so,
a woman I'll want, who will want me.
Surprisingly, though my candle is lower each day,
I'm confident, I suppose.
Empty now, with love lost many times, a fussy man,
I'm lucky to want,
    to sit in an easy chair in the City of Red Dust
    in the gated Friendship Hotel,
    to return from my impassioned lecture on heroic Walt
    and know myself Walter with some rooms in Brooklyn,
    to assume the world, the mud under my bicycle.

Oilcloth Covered Tables with Potted Flowers

After supper I am talked out. The moon is yellow
and has forest of stone hands
that keep it from singing.
After drinking sweet wine and digging into Mongolian
                    hot pot,
after euphoria and shaking hands with the cook,
I'm outside the red building with Wang
                    who reminds the moon
of her old drinking companions, Li Po and his shadow,
who jumped up to a river of stars.
I'm all talked out. The rusty gate drifts
around the compound like a fisherman lying in his boat,
wandering in a peaceful garden lake
others call the soul. The moon's hands are green.
I've one less day in my life.
The old school's locked up, the city closed.
It's only eight
but a Buddhist flute works up to heaven.
Soon I'll be back in my chair, trying to turn
                    into books.

At the Moscow Restaurant by the Zoo

We meet outside the gate to avoid signing in.
"I am Chinese," you say. I'm more comfortable
tonight than any night in China.

We eat at the Moscow Restaurant near the zoo,
in the foreign part, Old World and quiet,
where you can't go alone.

The stroganoff is cold but good. We don't drink
alcohol. They close early and we're out
by the big-character posters

in Beijing's first winter freeze. No taxi
so we walk to a nearby hotel you can't
enter without me.

'This is China,' you remind me. We talk
for three hours. I'm happy, sip hot water
and eat pinguo pie.

Your eyes couldn't keep staring at me
with laughter, with doubt and elegance,
if you'd not been *sent*

down to the countryside. We're back
outside on enormous streets. I don't
feel guilty for being

a foreigner. I'm not. We walk in Beijing's
thumping cold wind. I know the crowds,
I'm at home. I don't

want to leave one day. "We'll meet when
I'm back from Manila." You're translating
Kafka's letters

to his sisters. "Don't talk about my plans
or I'll lose my job." After nine o'clock
in the city there is

no place but people. It's a rich night,
better than one day when we're not
in danger. We find a cab.

The driver likes us and charges half fare.
We're slaphappy people, all of us roaming
through faith. Back at the gate

you keep the cab. I'm about to bang on the window
to say a last word. The cab pulls off. I know
you'll call in the early morning.

With Bei Dao and His Painter Friend in a Place Halfway Down a Hutong in South Beijing

Last night Bei Dao (who braved those years of writing
        for "Freedom Wall,"
who enjoyed wide readership by the Secret Police),
a young painter and I were shivering
in the artist's room in Beijing's coldest December
        of twenty years.
I warmed up by drinking hot water.
The poet and painter went out for wine so we could be
Persian
and mix alcoholic dream with our smoke.
In this city of hidden artists
we all pontificated and were profound.
Listening to Bei Dao so many dynasties patient,
hearing a scratch Beethoven sonata tape he put on for me,
I was honored and restored
by our elegant poverty, by books on the cold floor.

Bright Morning in Beijing

On our first night we sing all night in our sheets,
but as daybreak illumines orange cranes,
its needles of fire cross the city

and pierce our silky window. You worry,
ask me to leave first, walk down the stairway
and wait in the lobby of the Peace Hotel.
But I can't find the door to the stairs,
openly take the lift, it doesn't matter,
and we walk out together,
down Gold Fish Alley to Wangfujing
where my favorite Uighurs sit on the street railing.
In their tough-guy 1930s caps and striped suits
they raise my spirits. We take a narrower street
toward breakfast at the Beijing Hotel,
and it begins to snow. First snow in Beijing.
Bicycles slow down. We feel like gods
dancing on the whitened street. We issue happiness
to the blue figures who walk around us,
enjoying our joy.

China Songs

1

Chinese half moon, piece of jade,
a bowl of rice to feed the stars,
out in the West you were a gambler,
putting a new face on each night.
Here I take you back to my room
and sit you on my bamboo sheets.
You kiss me. So I wake from
being awake. One day they cut
off my hands and I wasn't even
a guitarist. You kiss me whole.

2

Why do I love you? I wrote you
a secret letter. And you sent

me cinnamon apple pie and words
I had no glasses to read. And soon
we were lovers. Yes, in China,
where love is ancient as lions
sleeping out in persimmon wind.
Will you ever leave me? I knock
on the door of the rain. We run
back into the mist to be alone.

3
Are you really bored? You gaze
at the fruit wagon like a gazelle
in Sinai baffled before a Hebrew
verse carved into the desert hill.
Don't worry. We're all just wise.
You took the train and I met you
on a sunny spring day. Isn't that
everyone's dream? Don't you know
one day we'll all descend into
Yellow Springs and live forever dead?

4
Don't be unhappy. Time is good.
So good each second we are breathing
bread. What's a little despair to
the orange tiles of a long dynasty?
China is more than a plate. My Greek
friend wrote that wherever he goes
the marble wounds him. How lucky
to be ancient! China is a world
of one woodcutter in the mountain,
O hermit, yes thunderously quiet.

5
You're good. This is the good night.

I'm jumping out of my sky because
you're so warm. Don't abandon me.
We slept alone for centuries.
I put on my shirt, took your hand
and found what sleep alone never
gave me. You. We were born alone
from night into gold. I've waited
all blood long. It's easy. I sing
and gamble, lost in our jade moon.

A Few Miles from Laos

I go from village to village, an outsider
looking for truth. It's a friendly morning
        to find nothing.
In the temple the newly made Buddha doll
dominates under its fresh orange paint.
I'm looking. It smiles forever saying nothing.
Artillery booms from the border region.
Clouds and a mountain of silk cotton trees
move upside down in the glassy rice water.

There are no Hans in this Dai village.
During the Great Cultural Revolution
the Han cadres ripped out the faces of the Buddha
but new faces are back on the altars with newly woven
        prayer streamers.
Dai women are thin like bamboo.
They wear peacock sarongs, silver belts and white
        straw hats,
even when working barefoot in the fields.
Pigs lumber, nosing for food before the rebuilt temple
where young saffron monks are playing cards.
I've no idea who was the master of the old master

in his kingdom on the bench,
who smokes his bamboo pipe while scrawling
a Hinayana prayer in Tibetan script.

Paddy water is a mirror for pristine forests.
The water buffalo, meandering, drop huge blops
of shit on the priestly road.
Again the thud of heavy guns.
The Hans and Vietnamese are still killing each other
          at the border.
I go from village to village, looking
for a translation of things into thought.
What do two morning moths have in mind,
chasing over the cabbage?
          Paddy water is a mirror
but without words to inform.
The sunny morning lasts two hundred years.

The Tree of Life

Don't cry for me. The tree of life
is full of birds. When I was old
in winter, lonely as a knife,
and when my heart was blue and cold,
I fell in love. Don't cry for me.
The tree of life is lilac blue
and smells of May and poverty,
poor as an orchard of bamboo.
I fell in love when I was young
and now I'm crazy once again,
in jail with jasmine on my tongue
and in my heart a cyclamen.
Don't cry for me. I'm young again
and every spring is cyclamen.

Spring Is

Spring is. I guess my life is still
a glance at resurrection. I've had
my share of winter. With no will
or fear at all, I eased from sad
and hollow to your Burmese thighs
slender and frank like the new moon,
and wondrous. When I kissed your eyes
of darkness, I knew sun, a noon
of accident. We plan. Spring is,
though you have flown to Dunhuang caves
to look at paintings. "I will miss
you," and you went. A season gave
us life. I wonder: Are wound
or lost? It's dawning underground.

Overcast

Look in your soul, O love. She's green,
and overcast and raining there,
her cows float up from a ravine.
You see as far as everywhere.
Be still. Look in your soul. Be still
inside as Adam's sleep, and hear
your hobo eyes under a hill
of dream. The dirty spring is here,
the Beijing alleys overcast,
a hutong court of memories.
You look for home. Strangely a past
of barn, of island and Greek seas
shows in the rain. I share your blow
of mist. It's raining in your soul.

Season of Falling Out of Stars

Spring takes a year and then it hurts
because I'm incomplete, which is
how you feel too. I let my shirts
pile up, swear I'll wash them, yet fizz
away like coke, can't clean up. For
some other time I say and dive
behind a book down on the floor.
I flop but Oh you're still alive
and I'm alive. Blood on the snow,
car bombs and a Tibetan shot
mumbling a prayer but you are not
a TV ghost. How prison slow
your coming was! My love for you
dresses a gulag in nice blue.

Trash Cart Mule

As I near my school gate, just another worker
on my bicycle, used to dodging death,
sharp in sniffing out coal from dung in drizzling rain,
late again yet proud of being Chinese,
I pass an upturned trash cart
and brake because its mule is waiting stiff,
a splattered statue,
garbage hanging on it like rippings from an ancient
             codicil.
The driver on his knees, sweeping, ordinary
in his hurry to amend, ignores the small crowd.
I can't stay to watch
but the incident is perfectly serious. It is
a chronicle of minor calamity
and a test of moderation. I leave the small crowd for duty.

The incident is closed,
no time to see the resolution and clean-up
of the animal and street,
of the resurrected driver and his patient mule,
its eyes bulging yellow with sun,
trash hanging on its black hair like wasted garments
from the mighty Qin Shi Huangdi.
Standing half naked, mere staring mule,
it is more alive
than all the emperor's terra cotta generals and stallions,
dug up and exposed to light,
who, from their open tomb at Chang'an,
glare straight ahead in eternal boredom.

The Great Wall of China

Most of the Long Wall—as the Chinese call him—
       is a ruin
and almost as old as Plato's beard.
Walking in the north I see him suddenly crawling
       into a poplar valley,
flashing through turquoise fall.
On a hill he has gold rings like the fingers of a god
       in armor.
He spreads as a great river
of stone against Mongols and Manchus—beautiful
       as a sunflower
and useless.

Another wall, of equal grandeur, snakes around
       my hotel and university,
snooping outside the huts of strangers in the hutons
and next to friends in their guarded flats.
He is ugly

and sinister as an informer's notebook.
Often, even in the raw sun battling into the haze
                    over polluted cities,
he is invisible,
and like a scorpion in a shoe or a rat on their chest
my friends in blue coats fear him.

On rare days when the Secret Long Wall is merely a ruin
sterile and dried up by the moon,
you my closest persist in seeing his watchtowers
                    and telescopes
as an astrologer sees gold typhoons blowing among
                    planetary rings.
On these benign days I phone you,
but you fear passing through his gate to my room
as if you were still Mongols and Manchus, Tibetans
                    or Uighurs
outside the stone eyes of the erect dragon.

The wall is heavy, omniscient, everywhere
so your feet are tattooed and turned to stone,
and I'm like you—foolish, cowardly, sane and streetwise.
Who can walk against the Great Invisible Wall?

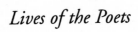

Lives of the Poets

Catullus

Your Catullus hates and loves, and is a friend to many
        Romans. Take that stinking rogue Victius.
His hideous mouth makes the farts of the foulest goat
        seem like honey, or Gellius the flasher,
his tunic open all night to his mother, or Lesbia,
        whose love I beg. Lesbia, I'm game
to journey to the trenches beyond civilization,
        to far India, to the barbaric Rhine
and even across the seas where the hairy Britons
        live in rainy isolation. But all
know that Catullus, with his Tivoli estate
        and Sabine refinement, is doomed
in Rome, since Lesbia (between noon and midnight) kisses
        the thighs of a hundred pin-brained
imperial lovers. The flower of my love, for whom
        Catullus would weep if even
her sparrow were lost, lies at the edge of the field,
        nicked by the plow. Since we are
viciously the same, I forgive us, and fire
        depriving me of reasons says
I want her. Yet there is someone of my own blood
        I love more, will not abandon,
and I journey to the East, to the continent
        where Jews and Philistines contend.
Alkaios found his brother Antimenidas alive,
        his sword ivory and gold. He fought
alongside the Babylonians, six centuries ago,
        came home, but you, my brother,
now are mere ashes under marble. I came too late.
        I offer funeral lentils, recalling
years we piddled away. Though you can't hear,
        take this plate dirty with tears,
saying, in perpetuum like the sun: Goodbye.
        Brother, hello and goodbye.

Alone in China with Du Fu

Du Fu, I keep meeting you on Boiled Rice Mountain
when the rest of the hemisphere is asleep
or making love or working in an all-night corrugated metal
        factory.
You fled officials under their umbrellas
and enjoy your sorrowful exile.
You watch the candle waste away in your room,
waiting for the gold lock to turn—will it turn?—
for the moon to hit the rafters of your cottage.

You scratch the scant hair on your white head,
look for a hairpin, utterly sad,
stealing life for your old age. Yet rain
falls into your courtyard as through childhood.
It falls on your daughter whom you sing
into twilight. With all your talk
I notice on the Mountain of Boiled Rice
you still wear your bamboo hat at noon.

Izumi Shikabu Talking from Her Pillow Book

Read my diary. I don't care
any more who knows
why I hate my pillow,
a moon smelling of you
like memory of oranges.

I woke in my young life
on a road of darkness
I can't walk to you.
Bells from the mountain
say I am utterly lost.

146

I'm sorry you suffer too
yet how glad I am!
Like bamboo I'm everywhere
as you wear out
the night with my face.

Prince, here in this world
my bed is ready
for scandal. What else
is there? With you
I'll lie down anywhere.

Is the moon in jail
since it obeys
laws? Each night
I hear great hail dropping
wildly from the moon.

I'll go to you by
horse and no one
will guess I'm mad.
If you're not there
I won't die tonight.

In some places they kill
lovers. A sweet story
for poets. Don't worry.
I hunger and am safe,
even if they destroy me.

Someone may gaze at stars
after you and I
are burned by the temple.
Be calm. We'll meet
so stars will remember.

Marie de France: The Moor and the Jew

Although I live in England where
The Roman vineyards now are bare,
I am Marie de France and write
In French of lovers and their plight
Under the angry gaze of those
Who'd turn to thorns their secret rose.
This convent with its eighty nuns
Suits me despite its tasteless buns
And mush the English think is food,
For I am free and never brood
Except when I recall grave pain
Suffered by two good souls in Spain.
My lay is drink for nuns and France
Who lack the milk of tolerance,
And Spaniards still revere these true
Adventures of a Moor and Jew.

Alphonse the Wise wrote many songs
In *cristiano* about the wrongs
That may be righted when the soul
Wakens to virtue and the mole
Of evil crawls back underground.
One day in court, hearing the sound
Of birds echoing in the street
He had a vision: soon he'd meet
Two heathen singers with the grace
Of nightingales, and like lace
That jewelers weave, their words
Would imitate the gold of birds.
Amazed he thereupon devised
A plan to find his dearly prized
Vision. Through contest he would bring
Those alien angels here to sing

To lords and ladies of his court.
Beauty and wisdom thus he sought
To teach the people of his city
Who needed lessons in true pity.

When the king's word spread end to end
A Jewish *moza* and her friend,
A Moor, were hiding in a grove
Of olives where they knew their love.
Of different creeds, just there could they
Be happy, could they talk and play
And chant, for yes, the nightingales
Were Sara and Zaïde, two sails
Of morning on a sea of fear.
Their friends and parents wouldn't hear
Of their affection. So they had
To act like strangers and be sad
Though they were filled with energy
And young. Their dream was to be free
And when the king's word came one day
Of course they knew they'd win. The way
To freedom lay in their sure fame
As favorites of the court. Their name
And gold they'd carry in their cape
Till one good night they would escape.

Who knows who is the villain of
This tale, who spoiled the perfect love
Of two rare souls destined to soar,
Of a fair Jew and her fair Moor.
Was Christian envy of their song
To blame? Or parents who could long
For only singleness of creed?
You choose the villain, reader. Feed
The foolishness of caste with rage

And ugliness. You have the stage
On which the next act came to be.

The saviors of false piety
Offered the couple a dark brew
To give them courage to get through
The tournament of song. Before
The king and clergy, on the floor
With emerald robes and diamond hair
Stood Sara and Zaïde. They drank
The altered brew. The courtiers sang
In silence, for they all had heard
That soon they'd know those golden birds
Whom none before had heard on earth.
Then as they waited for the birth
Of ecstasy, the couple tried
To sing, but since their tongues had died
Nothing was heard but courtier tears,
Alfonso's gasps, and covert cheers
From those who murdered them. Dear friends,
This tragic tale of lovers ends
Where it began. Some drops of glory
Fed two green trees. That blessed story
Of song was hushed and no one learned.
We're back again. You who have spurned
Marie de France's ancient lay
Repeat its misery today.

Chaucer's Tale of a Knight and a Rose

A glowing knight cantered through Lombardy,
Who was a chanticleer of courtesy,
Who in a lady's company was meek
And pensive like a martyr, who would speak
Of nothing but was upright, wise and good
As if he'd spent his manhood in a wood
Of nightingales and fawns. So kind his name
When villagers were threatened by a flame
Of vengeance from a despot, they implored
The knight for mercy and the gentle lord
Would cool the passions with his caring ways
And wondrous skills, and with a candid phrase
Of sound and sense made the protectors cease
Abuse of villagers, and there came peace.

One evening as the knight studied the sun
Descending to those hills where neither nun
Nor alchemist had ever gone to test
The soul and sod, he halted and took rest
Beside a garden that was rich in light
While eyeless darkness lay outside. A sight
More startling he'd not seen in marble Rome
Or Alexandria. There he found the home
Of a white rose who was a source of joy
And secret fear. The flower was wisely coy
Yet gazed at him who stole inside, but soon
Beside the rose a monk shone in the moon
That kept the apple trees awake. "What are
You doing in my yard?" "I'm lost and far
On a fair pilgrimage to anywhere
For Christian love, and now I merely care
To bow my head before some holy site."

At this the monk was wary of the knight,
Of foul and stinking deeds he might perform.
So thought the scabrous monk. "I do inform
You," he replied, "I'll fetch your bread and wine,
But in an hour I want you gone." "I'll dine
O happily with you," countered the knight,
Yet while he spoke his secret heart was bright,
Conceiving the young rose in all her beauty,
And swore to God he would obey his duty
To liberate the flower. Although he could
Not read, he knew he'd wandered in that wood
Because some higher word compelled his way
As once a Florentine (Dante, they say
Was his true name) was also lost, and found
A rose of fire moving the stars. The sound
Of dishes woke him from his reverie.
"Eat!" the monk roared, and left. The knight would see
The flower and tell his heart, and when alone
With her, he said, "Soft rose, there is a stone
Crushing my soul. Unknown, I've grieved my life
To be with you. If you will be my wife
Tonight, no force will ever separate
Our spirits." The flower was mute. It is my fate
To flee with you, she thought, and yet I know
Nothing of time beyond the gate. "I'll go,"
She seemed to say, bending her stem, yet feared
This night might rip her from her bed. Now cheered
In ecstasy, the knight reached for the rose and tore
Her from the earth. She issued fire. A roar
Of anger deafened them as her crude master
Discovered them. They fled, galloping faster
Than falcons racing out of a gale. "We're free!"
The knight informed his rose, and by a tree
They slept, knight and white flower, and his blue sword.
That evening as they slumbered the earth was gored

With joy. The severed rose dreamt she
Became a dame, and both perceived a sea
On which two lovers sailed on honey winds
Beyond this globe of kings or priests or sins,
Yet heartless time labored against their lot,
Condemning her, rendering him distraught,
And soon their joy lay vanquished in the mud:
Her petals dry, his blade concealed in blood.

Kabir the Wanderer

I can't weave in Benares. They threw me out
and many villages and towns say,
Go away, mystic of no caste or religion,
you are like the nameless animals.
They are right.
My sisters are Muslims and Hindus who have lost
their names.
I carry a lamp. At night my lovers show me their breasts,
their loins, their hair.
None has the word of Allah written on her.
None has a Veda chanting in her soul
yet we share the joy of the dumb beasts.

At dawn the sun is a gentle pearl
nameless as we were when we came through the great door
of being
or when we leave by way of darkness.
Kabir says: There is no place for words at death
when planets drop through our fingers.

I, Pierre Ronsard, Trembling in My Meadows

My name, Ronsard, is like a brooding rose
        Enduring the pink blasts of Mars,
        And Pierre, a suffering stone, is stars
        Born in my heart where nothing grows.

Yet poet of dawn, dark in a field I see
        A single lily with her crescent bowl
        Filled with the oil of France. I loll
        in panic by a hazel tree.

My mouth is sealed. I cannot even write
        These verses out of fear of her,
        My childish dream in time's quick breath.

I freeze before her breasts, her ankles white
        Moons on a holy green. I cannot stir
        a step till beauty cedes to death.

In a Letter William Shakespeare Says Who He Is

The worms have fed on blood, the dust has dried
The canticles of flesh, and time has coughed
On the brown marble of my throat. I died
But once. In that deaf fall down to the soft
Ice of extinction or to excrement
In the earth's tripe and carbon where a smell
Of former spirit haunts a firmament
Of coal, I'm free of Shakespeare's body and
His world, of heaven his unnatural dream
Against biology, of phoenix blood
His talking ink, and hover in a land
Invented constantly like sun or hell
Or love. But I'm in you. Like new spring mud,
Alive in you who make my maggots gleam.

George Herbert to His Lord

I wrote a letter to my Lord
But couldn't spell the holy Name:
"What can I do against the Sword
Lost in my flesh I cannot tame?"
The Lord answered (although I never
Posted my word to Him), and said:
"The Sword is nothing if whenever
You rave with Lust you let the lead
Of Heaven's glass be cut and crazed
So Light will magnify your Soul."
I sealed the letter and was dazed
Before my Lord who filled the hole
Made by the Blade with Angel Breath
And cured me with an early death.

I Andrew Marvel Offer This Elegy to My Companion, the Blind Secretary of the Commonwealth, John Milton

Milton, you are not gentle, for
You use a sledgehammer to roar
Against the gelid walls of Hell
Or crack the crystal citadel
Of Heaven, but to me you are
An age's soul and her wild myrrh.

I see you fumble on the grass,
Seeking your saint. You let her pass
Into your arms but then you woke,
She fled, and once again the yoke
Of solitude fixed you in night,
Though in your sorrow came a light.
Glowing from Eden, a green place

Below the shade of that live space
Behind the desert orbits of
Your eyes: a golden night of love,
With lanterns for the stubborn mind
Of freedom, where no one is blind.

There, my dear Milton, friend of shade,
Who nearly kissed the axe's blade,
With your dead eyes you held the sun
Of outraged Samson, bent and done
With noon. I moved your hand until
Came Mr Gout; your hand grew still.

I find my heavens in some ripe
Luscious apples, and melons wipe
My mouth with wine. I stumble on
A paradise, a virgin's dawn,
Under my feet. In my scant verse
Throbs my small garden's universe.

You dwell upon the handsomest
Of angels, outlawed Satan, blessed
And later cursed, your hero in
A sapphire world. Where you have been,
the golden lamp under the Sea
Helps God find His eternity.

Thomas Traherne on Earth

How Lucky was my Birth!
My Mother put me on a Blue, Green Pearl
          Which Atlases call EARTH
And left me on this Temperate Star to curl
          Into a Child
Of Bright Felicity, Roaring and Wild.

I came on Grass, a Tree,
On cottages with Luminous Walls of Glass
            Where shone ETERNITY
And yet amidst this Bliss I couldn't pass
            Above the Sun
to be at the Sweet Source where lives No One,
            No One but Dame White ROSE,
The Bloom who was the Mother of my Soul.
            White corn her Bed, She chose
To be Remote, Invisible, a Goal,
            a Sabbath Dream
For us thirsting the Waters of her gleam.

            And so I wept and grew
And angrily became a Man. My heart
            Was Iron; Lead my Shoe
Which sank me into MUD. I was a Cart
            Of Dross, and Free
Only to see Dead Wheels of Misery.

            After a Thousand Years
In Ponderous Clothes, my Mediating EYE
            Failed to glimpse other Spheres.
My Spectacle was an Abysmal Stye
            Of Pigs, my Home
The vomit of a Sea of Stinking Foam!
            And so I turned my Gaze
to the Lost Child inside who Nothing knew
            But Living Placid days,
Who fed a ROSE on Mountain Pools of Dew
            From Eden's Book.
Nothing he knew, and soon the Pages shook.

I read the Lettered Tree
Of Life and found no Words, but Unafraid,
With Earth's Lucidity,
I fed the Loving ROSE Deep in the Shade
Of the Dumb Soul
And as a Child I danced about my hole.

Basho

I write no last poem.
Dreaming thin rain on bleak hills,
Each line is my last.

Sor Juana Inés de la Cruz Who after Criticism
Gives Away Her Vast Library and Tends Her Sister Nuns
During a Plague until She Too Is Its Victim

When I am dead they'll say I was a muse
and praise my science and the poems condemned
by fulminating bishops who abuse
me as a bastard child, mestiza blend
of Indian criolla. Monks scrubbed the floor
two weeks to cleanse the profanation of
the prelate's house, for I (whether a whore
or nun), a female, tread his realm of love
for God. The same men beg our bodies, rage
if we refuse, and fume if we give in;
my secret love only in verse is heard.
They flattered me, painting me young, but age
is not deceived. Shade, dust, cadaver win.
Gone are the books, my loves and my stained word.

Arthur Rimbaud

When you are fifteen you wander far
on blue summer evenings through a wheat field,

scratched by the brush, your naked neck
bathed by the fresh air. Like a Bohemian

you go far on the paths, through nature,
happy as if you were with a woman.

Later you put your muddy boots on Madame
Verlaine's white marriage bedspread,

sleep with her husband, stab a Parnassian
poet in the hand, and when you wake,

embracing dawn you see a minaret
at the bottom of a well, cathedrals

in a lake, angels in pastures of emerald
and steel. You are a child mystic.

You are God. Verlaine charms and
revolts you with his human weaknesses,

but you write scriptures. The unknown
demands inventions: the new.

After a season in hell—you the infernal groom
with the foolish virgin—after your hunger

to climb a tower and weep in green mist
and hazels and invent vowels and wait

for the time when love seizes, and dine
on rocks, coal, iron, air—O happiness

O seasons O castles! After the tenderness
of impossible eternity, the sea

mixed with the sun, you ceased to be God
and measure your disgust with flight.

No one sees you again after you leave
Cyprus and sail down the Red Sea.

You run a high fever—syphilis and inactivity.
In Zimbabwe a girl from the Harari tribe

lives with you for a year. You care for her
and are almost happy. You need money.

King Menelek of Shoa fleeces you
in gun running, but you make silver

on slave trading and believe in science
and your companion servant Djami.

It would be good to learn the piano,
maybe have a son fully educated to be

an engineer. The botany of Ethiopia
merits articles in savant journals.

Here in Harar you live with bad food
among rotten natives, no mail, no highway,

three on a camel, the climate good,
but your tumor is dangerous. After

atrocious pain you hire a caravan
to Aden, the horrible rock. "My dear

sister Isabelle, in Marseilles they cut
off my leg. I am completely paralyzed,

unhappy, helpless, a dog. I'd like
to go home for a while to Roche where

it is cool, but tomorrow I die. Please
send 3,000 francs to Djami. For you,

my love, I have assigned my last
shipment of uncut sapphires and tusks."

Antonio Machado in Segovia, Daydreaming as Usual of Soria, Baeza, and Sevilla

My window grins over the crypt of John
of the Cross's bones down in the cypress grove.
I'm living up the hill in a small room on
the Street of Abandoned Children. I keep a stove
under the round table, a blanket on my knees,
and each night scrawl till dawn, throwing away
the papers with their dream of orange trees.
The hunched lady scrubs my ashes off the gray
floor and toilet's red clay bowl. My cell,
the dream ground of a Chaplin-walking man,
has (like Saint John's cell) a cot, chair, and field
around for solitude. The Andalusian
fountains laugh blue. My eyes, a lost moonbell,
are grave and funny like an orphan child.

Wallace Stevens Examining His First Spring in France

Brussels is cold and its stone houses brown
Because winter has let winds crumble over it,
Turning a day cloud into an illusion of crows

But on my first day, my first life, in Europe
I chose France, la Douce France, and its green
Canopy of meditation over the hazel trees

That suits a man of seventy who has looked
Into books and around books in his Connecticut
Habitat, and at last asks to walk the fields

Of the invisible. Was I frozen all these years
Like a glittering black letter fixed by law
On a legal document? Was the innocent

Of measured paradise existing in colorful
Fact on the sandy circus of the spirit,
Yet never in the holiness of the wanderer?   .

Even now a scholar will say I only dreamt
Of a bridge at Avignon, of a river where cows
Waited close by for sun to feed their shade.

Will the scholar of one candle care for real
Berries that I discover amid the ferns?
No. He will say I am a creature of Hartford, Animal of lucid

melancholy with words,
Solitude and a single destiny of flame
On Monday dawn, and a beast who never went

Into the greenness of his meticulous dream.
He will say I am poor as the vulgate bricks
By my windows. He will say I am helpless

Like the shoemaker Böhme or the lens-grinding
Jew from Holland, Spinoza, whose stars were all
The World, who never left the hyacinths

Of Amsterdam. And he'll be wrong. I will claim
A new taste of coffee dripping through a grate,
Peasant bread, a blue franc note whose fine lines

Create a woman looking Greek, anciently free
And robust. But the erudite will laugh
Since he is scrupulously informed and claim

These very tercets false and not by me. How shabby
To test my passport against the Mancha of
Don Quijote, a glassy imagination, and Sweet

France. Yet I have won, and the reader knows
In this gentle instant we are walking *chemins*
Along the Rhône, born in a solemn glacier

At Valais, and in my palpable enthusiasm
For its transparent shape I have gone too close
And soaked my shoes on its spring muddy bank.

On the horizon I watch the crystal mind
Of the firmament setting gold down with sudden
Authority of sunrays in a windowless room.

William Carlos Williams Back in Puerto Rico

Well Jersey is still a yellow place
May comes to with rain washing

chickens and pots of flowers
and New England—delicate rust

and immaculate white beds—
but back in old San Juan

it's beautiful as a baseball
game or Spanish Jews—I had some

of their blood too—escaping
laughing from the Inquisition.

Here slums are magnificent
baroque and golden red stone,

and what makes me happier than
the Pleiades is the skinny rubber tree

with big boobs and milk under
the skin all out in my back

yard or up in the tropical rain
forest. There pines are friends

and cool even to cranky old men
named Alfredo or Carlos

who walk with shaggy nostalgia
like the poor ascending home

where they listen to the radio,
make love, and iron new clothes.

Ezra Pound from Rapallo

One evening in Milano when the coloratura didn't show,
Vittorio Gassman went up on stage and recited
Dante's last canto
    l'amore che move il sole e l'altre stelle
And he calmed and dazzled the opera public.
Who will recite me?
After the fragments of fire and confession of failure
   in last canto 120
I vowed silence,
And near Syracuse I disappeared, dumping Laughlin
And the rest of the loyal gang.
The car roared after me till they found this silent
    gray dog meandering in a side street.
I'm only a bother now.

I've slept in many hired rooms.
Back at Wabash I stuck it out for a night
   in a Hoosier armchair
So a blond circus girl could snooze in my soft bed.
For that kindness they tossed me out
   of their midget male academy,
But Wabash kicked in a year's wages
And I went to London to help visionary Willy Yeats
Get his poems together
And to Paris where I wore an emerald in my ear
   powder in my hair.
There I let William Byrd handset my first cantos.
Byrd ended up in Tangier with one vellum copy
   and a small print shop
Next to a Spanish bordello.

Cathay was my red dream.s I picked up in London,
By suppering and gabbing on Thursday evenings

with young Sir Arthur Waley / Wizard of the Orient,
(né Arthur David Schloss), one of them Jews.
To the Chink poet Li Po, I gave his Jap name Rihaku,
        Englished him, made him my best verse
        since the Tang.

Meanwhile the Jews (whom all my buddies—Irish Willy,
Old Possum, Wyndy Lewis, even low-brain cummings—
        viscerally despised),
The Jews served as fine Fagans or pneumatically blissful
                        Viennese sluts
To color my quatrains.

I took to the old Greeks,
The glare of Odysseus stained with brine,
washing about the grape-white-porpoise surf,
        swimming into the rising twilight!
When her roseate forests turned moon-dark
I took to Artemis and the great gleaming disk of white
        cheese
She and her lions carried down from the summits.
But Roosen*velt,* the Dutch Heebe, ignored my letters
And pushed America into his world war.
I was a fool, saying rubbish on the radio. I repeat.
Yes, Elizabeth B would be right about me,
the old bad madman
        babbling in the madhouse.

I sat at my typewriter in Pisa, a nigger guard
        outside my cage,
And wrote nasty obscure crap about beauty,
About kikes and Jefferson,
And they showered prizes on me for it.
It got me out of the second cage, back to Italy,
Where I surprised them wops

166

As I wobbled down the gangplank to give them
　　　　the true Fascist salute.

Will someone recite me as Gassman did Dante? Today
They even like Whitman. I loved words
　　　　　　　　more than people.
My hatred created. It is not all rot
though Borges said, "Pound, one word for him, *fraud*."
In Portugal the cows meander amid the cork trees.
Across the river the Valencian girl of eight
　　　　came out to sing
In the afternoon when no one but a child
Dared to mention the name of the Cid.
I was always mentioned. I was a fool:
Finding hash ships I shipped out at daybreak,
Brave as a Saxon sailor.
When others lingered on their Victorian settees,
I, hearing the cock of Provence, its gold throat,
And sirens who sang through the ears
　　　　of irrepressible lovers,
I set out too
From Idaho, with a bad tongue fixed on beauty.
Vowed now to silence for my *peccati*, for gringo
　　　　vulgarity and bad verse,
For colossal errors I beheld
Only after the cantos finally petered out,
I die bravely in Wopland.

I, T.S. Eliot of Missouri

I

We are born with the dead. Not in a graveyard,
For graves conflict with sempiternal reality of frost
And fire outside my father's house in Saint Louis
Where I was alive, quick like sap, an urban tongue rising
        in May
With voluptuary sweetness.
We are born with the specter of the rose,
Who is color growth, whose word is decay,
Whose hope is interminable fire, now, and in time.

II

Sun is in the poplar trees, and in the mountain
The fog is memory in the fir trees, extending a cry
Of agony, of yelping seas, when prayer is no help
To those in ships, to those who would communicate
With Krishna or with Mars. I wonder how I came
To leave the Midwest for a polar island,
To live a routine of recalcitrant words,
To yield to passion, passion of a wasted youth,
To be the flesh
And dissect and abhor the bulging flesh
And despise those who squat in the shadow of desire,
Who incorporate the flesh in their sex and race.

III

But now in my freedom I discover the imperfections
        of time itself,
Which arrives at its station before the train,
Which invisibly reveals, in one flash,
Fields of corn and everlasting glory,
Children in the apple orchard
And the garden that remains a useless secret of the night.

These imperfections, like the errant ink made precious
On a misprinted postage stamp,
Become the serenity of my caged life.

IV

Old men should listen to the fury of the fog.
It begins when the moon, incarcerated in its light,
Raises the unheard waters, smelling of drifting kelp,
Against the water-created cliffs of northern Maine.
It loosens the winter pine forests,
Insists on floating over ice ponds and frozen lakes,
And snow fields recovering from the dawn.
Old men of letters, the critics squeezing their lemons,
The dancer who halts before she cracks the still heights
Over the earth where she stands paralyzed in joy,
Old men have sniffed those birds of paradise
Riding in tribes, faster than a skiff,
And seen them disappear where they began.
The fury of the fog cannot be heard
And therefore I listen. I am ignorant of the trill notes
Of the blizzard and mists that gather in Scotland
Only to wake in London with bowler hats and scones.
If I were an old man at peace I would destroy
My peace and listen to the throbbing fog.

V

We are not born with the dead but with lilacs
Who know death but know the summer best.
I am conscious of a day in a stern wooden church
In Missouri, outside the city, in a village where Tom
And perhaps Harry and Charles, having left the pigs
       In the stye, have gone in
To look at the smoke rising by the pulpit.
The wind outside was recently in Moscow, in Hampshire,
In Westminster where it curled around the shoemaker poet's

stone,
And now I hear its wing talking
Through the irregular miracle of recollection.
I remember nothing. The voices of the wind
Are possibly inventions, and because I journey into nothing-
ness
I hear logs being sawn through and tumbling
In a red forest, signifying Fall and lumber.

I do not know whether memory is another god
But I clutch it. It escapes.
The bell clangs

Waking future memory again. But going nowhere
I arrive nowhere, and with that bonfire knowledge
Blowing out, coming back, I choose the way of childhood,
Its lavender incarnation, its show-me green ignorance
Of ash and flower.
And when I cross the Atlantic back and forth, and once
          again,
Through nights
Where no light illuminates the ordinary fog concealing
          the groaning surf,
I see nothing over the timeless waters
And I am a simple prisoner of screaming peace,
Of the darkness where I end,
Where there is still a smell of grapes in a small garden,
And where the rose begins.

Max Jacob the Day He Was Seized
by the Gestapo, February 24, 1944,
at the St. Benoît-sur-Loire Monastery

Picasso painted all night long. You slept
and when the Spaniard took the bed at dawn
in the small furnished room you shared, you leapt
back to the chair to scribble poems and yawn.
One bed and two young artists. You were poor
always. Then you saw light and moved your soul
in with the monks. You always played the fool
and wrote of butchers with binoculars,
dancing the streets of far Japan whose moon
had fleas. Your books shone in the *librairies*
of Paris—Max's *caves.* One afternoon
the *Gestapo* found you. Your monks tried to save
you. *J'ai ta peau!* you joked, mocking the lice
that bit you, bravely punning to the grave.

Osip Mandelstam and the Kremlin Mountaineer

You said his thick fingers were fatty worms,
His moustache huge laughing cockroaches,
And you caught him relishing an execution
The way a gourmet rolls a berry on his tongue.
Can you blame Stalin for sending you
Into hell? The train to Vorenezh
Was a lovely old ikon compared to the transit
Wagon that meandered with its insane,
Sometimes lucid, prisoner who wrote
Pleas for money and warm clothes on a scrap
Of brown paper. Somehow it got through.
Your heart kept graying and then stopped
But the guards in the stars of the Caucasus

Could not permit your death. They made you live
A while. How beautiful the steppes! The lips
Of the moon beamed against your teeth.
In your mouth you perceived snow-blue eyes
Of the heaven over Russia. In the camp
You went insane and slept in a red ice grave.

Mayakovsky at a Mexican Wedding

More people are killed
at a Mexican wedding,
they say, than in a bloody

                Mexican revolution.
But we just drink tequila

              until cactus swims

                        prickling our

brains,
and Diego Rivera,

           comrade

               and host of hosts

puts down his brush

            with white horses

                  springing

out of its thistles

           and starts to dance

                  Cielito Lindo

laughing,

           hotter than a heavenly plate

                  of tamales.
I turn as an oyster

           and remember onions

                  camping on the

Kremlin roofs.
I weep enough salt tears

to burst a fireman's barrel,
ponder lightning telegrams
                    I could send
to the Milky Way,
            to my French or Russian Jewish
                                love of
loves,
to the radish
            and its teeth living
                        inside the earth.
But crash,
while I plunder my life's boat
                    the wedding guests
begin to scream, insult,
                pull out ornate revolvers
and shoot at the sun!
                What happened to grace?
                                Is she
hanging with my trousers
                in the moon's green closet?
I, Vladimir Vladimirovich,
                am furious as a Lap
whose reindeer are about to be
poisoned.
        I can't speak Diego's Spanish.
                        How can I halt
the family war?
            Recalling Nijinsky
                        I leap,
the giant I am,
            between two fuming macho
                        wedding war-
riors.
I shout
        TOVARISCH!

and they stare at me
as at an old serpentine statue
of a green wrestler
gazing
from the shade halls of a Maya pyramid.
The rumpus stops.
I've shamed
and shocked away the *pistoleros.*
I'm hilarious. Diego says
I saved the battleship
of Mexico from being eaten
by an arum lily
floating up from
Mr. Bosch's Hell.
I'm so happy.
Will my huge
sad insulting bulk
again play Russian roulette?
Peace has erupted
out of blue Popacatépetl.
Now, my round Olmec friends,

be married
this noon of carnations
with lemon
in your hair. Soon night
in its tinfoil hat
will sing like scorpions
under the moon in her house
of feathers.
The incident is closed.
Let me leap back like a jade tiger
to my vodka
homeland,
dreaming of

time,
more time for childhood,
                        for Russian melodramatic love
and all my towering posters,
                    more time
proclaiming lucidity
                    like yellow ceramic domes
of churches erected and gleaming
                            over Indian corpses,
time for the Moscow domes where I store my clouds.

In matrimony
            I'll never know,
                        in Orthodoxy
I'll never claim,
                I pray for more
                            calendar time
lucid   like a whisky   under the impatient sun.

in Frogland i ee cummings

in Frogland *i* ee cummings
after a devil's island pimp weeps
& cons me in Club Venus
where one big signboard sighs
                        ON EST NU,
hire a hack (i relieve myself out the back)
but a flic nails me charges me
                        with crime
:vot ist meine crime, M. le flic?
Monsieur, vous avez pissé sur la France

i am young c'est paris la guerre est fini
ladies come from cambridge reds devour la russie

wops jews play with madame

      Death

and me froggy

    yank

in la belle France furiously drink onion soup
by the rivers of les Halles before
dawn's vegetable light
with ohsowearyladiesofthenight
who me wake

     to the bur-

den of being as criminal as villon ,broke as baudelaire
,springcrazy as my father geniusof joy
& *CALLIGAMMES*

       (& who's my oh! daddymaster)
GUILLAUME APOLLINAIRE

Last Voyage of Hart Crane

The rose tarantula is hanging from
The window of my Aztec house—the worm
Sleeps in the bottle of mescal—I come
Drunk as a white volcano—my dead sperm

Finds no black stars in hell—O Lord,
I'm on the floor!—the lily is my sun
Tricking me into hope—I am the ward
Of brutal bells that ice the broken dawn

With clanging nails of crucifixion—yet
In this bronze noon my old Indian friend
Affirms me mildly through the alphabet
Of resurrection—carillons offend

The pit of truth—I wake—O Lord—I wake
But not to azure dawn—how many nights
Must I ride with the hurricane?—The snake
I wear—the smutty serpent chills and lights

My tongue's despair—its campaniles and lutes
Shower me with glass—I see the firmament
Still green—Save me—I'm floating—Love pollutes
Eternity! Go home?—Pesos I've spent

On boys. Woman, receive me in your hands.
The belly of the Sea invites my gaze.
Snow lies on its rite moon—a kitten lands
On me—it gently cries for me. I praise

The Heaven of the Jews—let us the Weak
Find Mercy in her Sighs. Tomorrow when
I say goodbye to her, maybe I'll seek
A way back up when I have cast my pen

And me into the cruelly pious hope
Of waves. Or when my visionary love—
Our argosy—casts me to the caving rope,
Maybe I'll let the dogfish drift above.

Borges and His Beasts

Something is wrong with your face. No, it's not
an old man, but one who has not grown up.
Despite gray hair or one eye caved like a cup
and dead, and one eye that is a gray plot
of yellowish mist through which a white deer
leaps and fades or flashes blue in a dream
where you forgot your death, you longly scheme
the alphabet of light to fill the sphere

in your heart. Blackness gone, now you must smile
like a child. You relish an Old Norse word
offered the sky. But lonely and absurd
you know something is wrong. Face of a child,
laughing, tormented like a tooth, your eye
waters to know the panther who cannot die.

Love Song of Robert Desnos

for Youki

Yes, I am rarefied like wires that tie sunflowers
                around winter clouds
And feverish like the heat under mushrooms
When the forest around a Normandy village
Is smoking with a shipwreck below the eyelids
                of wild boars,
And still three days away from death in Theresienstadt
I stay alive because I dream you fiercely,
I dream you through the shade of carbon bayonets,
Through hills of stolen gold teeth and that wooden platform
                from which our friends are hanged notoriously
                in public, just for us,
And although my typhus spares me only these hours
                to send you a message through a Polish student,
I go on dreaming you as if my brain were made of marvelous
                steel arms
Which hold you and are held by you.

Think, I once said you were a herd of oxen
Remote from me, stopping indifferent, and you couldn't love
me
Even if I stepped through my passions out of the world
                into greater passions
And became a scholar of love, a diamond-eyed pedant

Footnoting my madness around a table of stars.
But then I hadn't had you, nor you me, and I hadn't had you
gone,
As this evil camp has made us gone—
Or so they thought.
And I am too weary now from camp fever to be anywhere
                but with you.

I have dreamt you in the mornings when the sun forget
                it was a flower
With a duty to feed us its aloof and imperishable beauty.
I have dreamt you at dusk
When airplanes dropped like sugar into coffee, spreading hope
                to the shackled.
And tonight I dream you, since I love you,
And even my blood, which is reluctant to dance through silk
                on its amazing adolescent merry-go-round
                (for I have run out of francs to drop in it),
My blood still whistles to you. Do you hear me?

I hear you fiercely and love you and quietly in the night
Though sun be weak and too slow to arrange with nightin-
gales
                and dawn
To hurry here bright with your face,
To carry your eyes, your throat to this now free camp
And reach me in time in my burning shade.

Miklos Rádnoti in His Overcoat Stuffed with Poems on Postcards to His Wife

Because time is a fiction in the mind
I don't want to die, that is, in July
Or Friday or last year. Farms and haystacks

Are burning today. I, Miklos Rádnoti,
Write you a poem on a postcard. Darling,
I say to myself I won't lie down. The ox
Drools blood. The shepherd girl is an orphan
When the troops stray over the wheat fields.
Wife, after they beat me to death, look through
My trench coat, in the roadside grave, for poems.

Maybe in two years, by 1946,
You will find our bodies. Today all over
Hungary and Poland I am dying. In tavernas
I am already forgotten. How could the smell
Of my hair linger? I hid in cellars too,
Smoked in darkness, kissed kisses of the taste
Of blackberries. When peace comes I won't be
At the Writers Club. Angels drink artillery.
Peasants drift among fleas, among worms. Wife,
The poems are time's wings. Spread them darkly.

Brick Song of Theodore Roethke

I call myself the dancing bear, and though
I'm big and blazing with a bleak desire
To lindy with a beauty—not some crow—
My truth, my skip through hell, is a gray fire
(Jakob Böhme saw in a pewter plate),
A dish of sunlight serving up my fate.

That wretched cobbler of philosophy
Gave me abysses and auroras too.
I swing between a mad felicity
And gobs of reverend gloom, the holy glue
That holds my squirming soul in one dark shade.
Each night I sew up holes, but I'm afraid.

Be close to me. I'm sick and shy and try
To dance my arrogance. A man's a bag
Of miracles that cynics call a lie,
Yet if I can't turn ashes or a rag
Into a rose, I might as well lie down
In a Long Island swimming pool and drown.

Dear sweet Beatrice, since Dante found your name
I stole you for my bride. You stole me with
Your swaying bones and we became one same
Slow rising butterfly We are the myth
Repenting from a dream of solitude.
I dwell there, fat with you and sweetly lewd.

Be kind. I want to live. I try to live.
While egrets whiten banks along the Nile,
Its sewers nourish me, a fugitive
From calm. I wear a golden crocodile
Under my shirt. It brought me you and day
When all hope drained into mere boring clay.

Under my shirt I am like all of us,
A nakedness that craves eternity.
Sometimes I sing or groan; I make a fuss,
Am caged a while until I learn to be
Easy again with you. Lord, let that flame
of horror bleach a bit, and I'll be tame.

Talking with James Wright

James, I could be dead too—we each chose
            to come up to earth

in the same year, yet you dropped early
            into the ground under

New York. I see you always at the beginning.
                    You were young, chanted poems

like a rabbi showing off dark truth, which grew
                    huge in the tavern.

Now you are caught in darkness and pulsation.
                    I hear us three decades ago,

dreaming loud in a New England village
                    about Peru, Spain, their poets.

A wild man in proper dress, you drank too much.
                    Over the beers in bad light,

you quoted Vallejo, "I don't feel like staying alive,
                    heart." What a lie! Even while

you lay in the hospital, you couldn't believe
                    such rubbish. You scrawled poems

on a small pad after they cut out your tongue
                    down to its cancerous root.

Histories 1992

Killers in London

In 1952 I went to hang out with friends in a flat
south of Chelsea, with drugs,
an American artist, and women sprawling on men,
all in a house where bodies
were buried in the walls. It didn't smell yet,
and none of us knew about the crimes.

After they picked up the London strangler of whores,
Christie the necrophiliac
sat in his cell and wrote letters to his old pals
about banalities while waiting
to be hanged. I kept up by reading the tabloids
in the tubes. His house south of Chelsea

had a nice garden. That afternoon when it rained
it smelled of dead animals.
Sam Francis the painter smelled it, but was too
doped up to care. He smiled.
If I were Buddhist, I'd be scared to come back.
The London haze held through the night

and in that dead pause just before noisy dawn,
Portuguese fishermen
strolled through the crooked alleys, looking
for brandy or a dive
to sleep off a drunk. Each sailor carried a bag
with necessaries and a suitcase of dry cod.

Back in my boarding house, before our landlady
brought in food, she examined us
contentiously. All of us were nervous at lunch.
We had the meat pre-cut,
serving it with mustard and watery salad,
and set the table only with spoons.

Federico in August

You were never calm
like the orange trees of glass in La Huerta,
in the sun,
and every terror, Federico García, went
into your poems.

You hid upstairs in
the Rosales house within sight of the police.
Your attic radio,
with word of arrests, executions, played
nationalist marches.

When the blueshirts
came, you were lost. They told Rosales lies
at the station.
And Falla came too late. By the next morning
when that devout

Catholic composer pleaded
for your life with the governor Valdés Guzmán,
Valdés said he'd
look into the situation but already had the
report of your death.

You were handcuffed
together with the Republican teacher and
an anarchist bullfighter.
They pushed you on your stomach
at the Fountain of Tears

where shots exploded.
Valdés had decided to give you plenty of coffee,
meaning lead,
and the blueshirts obeyed. After the volley
you got an extra bullet

in the ass for being
a queer. The Fountain of Tears has a grove of
olive trees. It was dawn
1936 when Spain lost its hand and you lay
by the dim roadside.

Antonio Machado at the Franco-Spanish Border

In 1939, Barcelona fallen
and blue troops advancing, Antonio Machado,
his mother, brother Joaquín, and

intellectuals jammed in a military ambulance
headed for the border. His party was
turned back, but told to cross a mile

north through the January snow. His friends
worried that the sick poet would die
of exposure if they sloshed north,

yet the poet insisted that he had time,
he had time. It was still snowing
when someone said the name *Machado*

at the guard house, and the French lieutenant
on duty recalled a poem he had read
by the Spaniard in his lycée textbook.

He waved them on across to Collioure,
the village where the Cubists painted
their first cubes. There Antonio, recalling

Sevilla, walked on the beach, and scrawled
his last line in a notebook, *Those days
blue with the sun of childhood.* His legs hurt,

Spain was gone. Dejected, fond of his French
landlady, in the light, he lay weary
on his hotel cot and died. He lies in France,

though his friend Juan Ramón Jiménez
wrote in 1957 that he had gone back to Spain
through the sky below the earth.

The Secret Reader   1996

Everyone is a secret reader. Every book is a secret reader too. And even in those apparently barren and lone caves at Qumran, hidden words on a papyrus apocryphon waited, as we all wait, for eyes to discover and decipher them. So, by accident or luck or the begrudging indulgence of time, the secret reader may find the secret reader.

—Pierre Grange, "On the Dead Sea Scrolls"

The Secret Reader

I write my unread book for you who in
a life or day will find it in a box
or cave or dead man's pocket or the inn
of mountain light where we awake while cocks
of twilight scream our solitude. Our fate
is to be free. No public ink. No hot
or cold inferno of the private wait.
Just this apocryphon which I forgot
for you, the secret friend. You are like me:
one soul fleshed out for ecstasy and night,
this planet's only birth and death, unknown
like everything. Saul lied about the light,
for no one rose again. We are alone,
alive with secret words. Then blackly free.

Gas Lamp, 1893

In brownstone Boston down on old Milk Street,
up two gray flights, near the gas lamp, the tailor
waits glumly for the midwife. August heat
has worn the woman out. Amid the squalor
she looks around the bed, clutching a cape
she brought from London as a child. It's dawn
and dirty. The dark tailor wants to escape
to his cramped shop. The woman's sheets are drawn
below her waist. She isn't hollering now.
Her eyes are dark and still; blood on her thumbs.
Her name is Sarah. No. I'm guessing. How,
untold, am I to know? Hot day has worn
into the room. The midwife finally comes.
Grandmother bleeds to death. My father's born.

Grandfather

Born over there, in mist, not even God
or Germans have a record of the house
or village outside Vilna. Here, the old
poor tyrant snips a cloth, stitches a blouse
or shirt, and finds a black woman to live
with when his wife is dead. His smart son sells
papers in Boston subways, won't forgive
the tyrant fool for whipping him. The smells
of steam and cooking mix with yellow cheeses
when suddenly the wrathful tailor seizes
a belt and flogs his son for rotten grades!
Last drama. Twelve years old, my father leaves
his home and school for good. The tailor fades
from all of us forever, stitching sleeves.

Mother Writes a Book of Breath

In innocence I piss and scream and wake
from belly-roaming seas, and pre-sperm death
is nine months gone! My first practical joke
is peeing on a nurse's face at this day-birth
of sleep on earth. That's life. My shit and stars
are all about, but arms of love sweep me
from loneliness. Mother removes the bars
of dungeons lost inside, kisses me free
of knowledge, free from the first union of
the blood. She writes a book of breath, page one.
I cry and she is near throughout the night
of infancy, feeding this alien love
with woman's milk. But now her breath and sun
are gone, and she moves into unknown light.

Father on Glass Wings

Death calls from Colorado spring. The phone
tells me you jumped: angel with dizzy stone
arms, floating on glass wings. But you don't land.
Childhood. We're selling watch straps, store to store,
sharing a shabby Greystone room. The floor
is spread with schoolbooks. As you take my hand
we ride downstairs for papers: SNEAK JAP PLANES
SMASH PEARL HARBOR!! I've got Latin to do
but we walk Broadway. Dropping through spring-blue
sweet air (I was in Brunswick's tedious rains),
you shattered in the gutter. You'd be gray
by now, I guess, and coming up the stairs
is my young son I love the same old way.
He can't see you. I won't know his gray hairs.

Bowdoin, 1948

Hawthorne once had this yellowed room. We share
the morning gloom of alcoholics or
nocturnal masturbators, north and nowhere,
too isolated for a date or whore.
Were you a grind like me? A dreamer slob
and weird? I sleep, the window open to
the black Maine snow, hearing my roommate throb
and scream, an epileptic getting through
another siege. He's a philosopher;
I'm lost. But he was born a bastard, he
says bitterly; my origins I shirk
from. Worst (or best?) I doubt there is a me
concocting words in terrifying blur
within. Dream, Hawthorne. Words no longer work.

Tropical White Pajamas

In Mexico in a poor village near
the live volcano with its summer snow
and smoking heart, the Quakers settled here
and I dug privies in the mornings. Oh!,
one evening in the streets of Vera Cruz
I danced, wore a green mask; we heard the wild
huapango song, big stars cooked us. Those loose
tropical white pajamas and the mild
faces of Indian friends soothed us. We went
back to our room, our bed, took off our clothes,
both innocent as Eve. The *patrón* laughed
at us, smirking. Dawn found our bodies bent
for the surprise and birth of light! Who knows
your name? We fished through white night on our raft.

Rocking on the Queen

Deep in the hold we have no porthole, yet
I gaze, X-raying whales and a green squall.
The pitching of ELIZABETH has set
the tables rolling, banging wall to wall.
I push up to the deck and wait for France.
At twenty I'm a character whom Plato
might keep for lunch—yet the Greek's reasoned trance
is not my Bergson dream. I'm a potato-
head says my Marxist pal. Norm's blind but grins
at me. Naive! As Europe nears, wet shade
washes my eyes with reverie. I dry
my face. Europe is full of women. Inns
of smart delicious lips. We dock. The maid
at l'Hotel Flore pinches my pants and tie.

La Rue Jacob, 1948

War was fun for Guillaume Apollinaire,
sending letter poems from the trenches, yet
a bombshell came, gravely combing his hair,
but Guillaume healed in Paris, a cigarette
like a love ballad in his lips. I spied
life from a hotel room with a red rug,
hot water in the corner sink, and sighed
happy when the street singers used a jug
to catch the hailing francs. The courtyard reeked
with rising fumes of piss when evening rain
fell from the wine-blue clouds. Our sheets were far
too short. 1918. Spanish flu streaked
through France. Gamins of his bohemian brain,
we missed Guillaume. He croaked with *La Victoire*

In a Paris Faubourg

My Polish classmate at the gray Sorbonne
loves the romantic poet Bécquer. She
wears heavy wool, is Chopin-thin and fun
in Paris rain. One night she secrets me
off to a grim Free Polish Army party
up in an orange room. We're comrades and
march behind banners down Boule Miche. Hearty
and generous in bed, she takes my hand
a Sunday morning; we go to a faubourg,
a sleazy house. I don't guess why. "It's clear,"
she says. "I'm pregnant and abortion's not
a legal act in France." Up in the morgue
the Syrian doctor cuts her up. "So, here
is your chef-d'oeuvre," he tells me. We are rot.

White Island

My first day at the school for Constantine
I meet a peasant father with two hooks
(wounds from Albania) and the German Queen
of Greece who loans me her blue *Faber Book
of Verse.* But soon I'm fired and so begin
to loaf and write on islands. Mykonos,
the iceberg. I'm the only *xenos* in
the village, living with a Greek, and close
to getting jailed for working without papers.
The ship comes twice a week. Down at the pier
we all watch who comes in, but lemon vapors
of broiling fish seduce me. One white night
Captain Andonis slaps his heels. Austere,
he teaches me to dance, to live on light.

An Andalusian Winter

It's early Franco Spain. Hunger of serfs
and fishermen like insects sleeping on
the sand under their boats. When morning surfs
into the village we pick up fresh prawn
and goat meat. Justo's all upset. They caught
and killed some *rojos* in the hills, and threw
the bodies over horses which they've brought
into the plaza on their way up to
the old Phoenician common grave of Jews.
Our farm—with sugar cane and orange trees,
with snow magnolias—is a paradise
for five *reales.* Lorca's a man of vice,
un loco to his fascist cousin who's
our mayor. Laughing I grieve by these old seas.

A Blonde in Tangier

Sean is an Irish Jew crossing on the ship
from Algeciras. He's just dumped his wife.
He has a snapshot of a Seville whore he whips
out in a flash, "She loved me." His bum life
with his old bag is over when her father socks
him. "No more fried-egg suppers." Sean pops by
one famished evening, saying, "Buddy, shall we wet our cocks?"
We go. A new moon stabs the virgin sky
over the Zócalo. Veils and kif fan the air
as we stroll eager through the Casbah streets.
Stores wide open. A narrow parlor jammed with Berber men
on *azulejo* benches smoking dope. The whores next door
    sit marketed on chairs.
"You first," says Sean. I choose a blonde. She treats
me fine. She's knocked up. Sideways I plop in.

A Tower in Tangier

Some place among onions of pain I lose
my nerve. Gone is the table in that tower
on the west coast of Africa I used
to climb to in the afternoons, where hour
on hour I'd smoke, sip tea, and look at ships
fall off the glass of fire into a throat
of stars. Back in my room a bone rat slips
along the walls, singing the infant note
of swallows as I boil the milky smell
of oatmeal on the green alcohol flame.
The green Casbah moon floats over the square
like a knife patient in the dusk. I came
to climb jail steps to you. The Moors in prayer
yell from the towers. I climb, crazed, infidel.

201

Hiding in a Wardrobe Closet from a Landlady
in London of the Great Fog

Winter mornings. London is dark. The fog
comes in the common toilet window (which
we're not allowed to shut). I read and hog
the quarters on my freezing buttocks. Bitch
and scrooge, I call Mrs Brightbottom who
leaves me her nasty notes. My lovely Thai
friend will redeem the day. I'd like to screw
her royally (I confess, ashamed, since I
am also dreamily in love with her
thin smile, her wistful arum lily throat).
The fog has killed the bulls at Hampton Fair
and I can't get to SOAS. Through the blur
I walk to Oussa's sheets. The night we share.
At dawn I'm hiding in her closet coat.

Boot Camp in Georgia

"Yeah," shouts the corporal, "all Jewmen fall out!"
A black kid and me, we go to pick up
our 3-day pass from Dix. "What's it about?"
"Jewish New Year." They fly us with our pup
tent, boots and duffle down to Georgia where
still on the airstrip a white sergeant blurts,
"Sound out your name and race!" We're in the fair
sweet South. "I'll squeeze that bastard till he squirts
white piss," the black kid whispers. I get stuck
three days on K.P. God what grease! I feel
good here. No anti-intellectual crap
of campuses. I catch pneumonia but heal
fast and they treat me good. Have friends and rap.
I don't have to kill. It's peace. What the fuck!

Yale

Sterling Library is a confession booth
where Virgil hangs out on a shelf by stars
gold on the ceiling calm and beaming truth
and blue blood aristocracy. Guitars
are out. I haunt the books, reading Jack Donne
who kisses metaphysically. In class
I'm shy and tongue-tied among gentlemen
and lovely women scholars. What a gas
to eat at Louie's, peddle to East Haven,
play with my infant daughter now become
my lifelong sun. With stupid discipline
I race through (gone for good the wandering bum
of Europe) yet among my peers I'm craven:
no pilgrimage to Ezra in his loony bin.

Red Guard Beijing, 1972

Madness is in the air. There is a smell
of progress from the fiery factories and
from *hutongs* and mass toilets. The death bell
of nightingales is heard throughout the land.
I wear my Mao button. At the opera
my comrade from Inner Mongolia informs
me that "this joint is really jumping!" Ah,
I am a fan. I catch the zeal. Reforms
have unbound ankles, freed the children hidden
in dark mills, cured the deaf. The once Forbidden
City is a museum. I'm at the zoo,
I boat romantically on the snow lake
where once the Summer Palace Empress threw
heads in a well. Red Guards keep death awake.

Sewing Up a Heart During the Cultural Revolution

Shanghai. I smell my fear among the smells
of medicine and patients in the hall.
The nurse ties on my mask, quietly impels
me toward the table, but I hug the wall.
Hard to witness the bloody cut mushroom
of a man's heart. The eyes are open as
he sips a bit of juice, and the perfume
of death drips off a nylon thread which has
repaired the shadow of a soul. His ear
holds one electric needle, quivering.
His eyes call out. I think about crazed Lear
carrying his daughter, drownings off Vietnam,
my coffined mother on the train. All being
is good. The dark and gentle night is sham.

Near Annapurna

We are still at cloud level. Beautiful day.
Thin air. Cold but our sweat warms us. The snow
jungle of rhododendron weirdly gray
around the deadly trail. My friend starts to blow
up, bitching, "Don't come too close!" A mule went
over the ledge an hour ago. We inch
down a stone cliff. ANNAPURNA. Indifferent
white continent. I can't make it. I clinch
the ice, crawl the ravine. As snow turns to mud
I slide on my buns. It's raining. Beautiful
hot rain almost washes us off the top.
We find a smoky cabin. I'm full of blood.
Go in feverishly filthy, dirty wool,
drink a pot of hot lemon juice, and flop.

Fever and Carnival in Vera Cruz

I'm seldom where I am. Herons and snakes
color the forest of the pyramid
where the old sungod dined on hearts amid
the stains of human fat. We climb. It wakes
the bell of absence, yet those days are gone,
the carnival in Vera Cruz, the flame
of dancing with a lover in the zone
of jasmine through the streets. Happy I came
to drink in your winevault. I'm seldom where
I dream. Off in the jungle, by a tree
waiting for revelation in the glare
of nature, till I wake to a simple cold,
a wobbly fever and the anatomy
of pain for being dreamy, empty, old.

The Camp near Kraków

Over the gate the sign ARBEIT MACHT FREI.
I guess my village outside Vilna, which
was razed, came here in cattle cars to die.
Today it's raining on the Kraków church,
its peaceful domes, and on the camp which is
a gray museum. I see the children's skulls,
the shaven heads of Jews and gypsies, Poles,
photos of eyes like prehistoric flies
stuck on the walls outside the shower room
in which the rain prepared the bodies for
the ovens and the sky where bodies bloom.
ARBEIT MACHT FREI. Auschwitz is mute, the war
already fugitive. The rains evoke
a Slav, black-hatted Jews, tattoos and smoke.

Inlight in Providence

Before the dawn in Providence, before
the crows, the garbage men step out. Their cries
crack the air like lone Basque shepherds. The roar
of stars behind the hills. Although my eyes
are closed, the providence of sleep is gone
and time hovers handcuffed to time. I'm not
ready to fade to opaque prison dawn
and wish to wade under the river, caught
in galaxies of kelp. The gas stove talks
to me, the wind gets up, my brooding locks
me on the lonely earth where I'm a dream
under a sky of mint stars. Garbage pails
are rolling down the street. In the extreme
daybreak I wake from waking. Inlight pales.

Recalling a Life with a Greek

September melancholy. You are there,
sketching the island of the moonhigh wheat
and enigmatic tides. The iron chair
out on the terrace with your form. You eat
the Euboian yogurt cured in sacks and drink
sage tea with honey which the hotel stored
for us. And sketch the chapel. As I think
about our hills, the cave and brook, the sword
of water glittering the pepper tree,
I sigh for us. A thousand years have not
erased your drawing. Hold the sun. The fall
of Thera and our ghosts are a white dot
before your charcoal eyes. Near that spring wall
we pause. You sketch the tombs of porphyry.

Theft of a Brother

My brother lives between Mobile and Gal-
veston, in a great villa like a rose
between two pumping oil wells. He's my pal
and by the pool we play at dominoes
and drink, gossiping until the garden trees
swallow the moon, the aristocratic plants
and poor bamboo, until the old disease
of love maddens our brains with jungle ants
biting the family blood, and we escape
by car and plane. I have gone back to Rome,
stunned by a grave of brothers and its rape
or rain chilling the plate of lentils left
for us, that hateful feast after the theft
of brotherhood. The rites have killed our home.

While My Daughter Is Sleeping

Brooklyn. My daughter sleeps on the main bed.
I have a couch next to the books, and lie
slanted but get to sleep. I've cut a thread
holding a swallow from the wandering eye
of fire. Under God's foot the cyclamen
is raging. Suddenly, there is no wife
or brother, sister, house. Clean day. Again
I start. Seferis wrote about his life,
"Let me grow old and die in my own land."
Can I grow old or die? Is there a place
my own? Child of N.Y.? White Greece? Black grace
of Patagonia? For each continent
I ache or laugh, but choose the ghostly hand
of the wind. Words, like flies, become my tent.

N.Y. Heat Wave

The light is all around us like a black
burning flounder. Below it black kids work
the hydrants, gunning cars with booming flak,
and cool the poison fish over New York.
The light is also *in* us, Hasid dark
and blazing in our brains down to glass trees
with roots of dream. I live from a black smirk
of unknown light, the ghost who never sees
herself yet knows the unknown universe
pulsing with supernovas. Angels sweat
and their wings drip with oil and steam and salt
into those Village junkie mouths who curse
at walls and retch darkly into the vault
of poison day! It's hot till we forget.

With My Redneck Sons in Southern Indiana

The pampas of America begin
north of our barn. Glaciers smoothed down the earth
for buffalo and corn, but I live in
the poor south hills where farmland isn't worth
the taxes, and the KKK comes out
of the wet Gothic woods. Our humpbacked barn
is rusty in the patient twilight. Scout-
ing the Blue River bendable as yarn
or glowworms, I am not quite Baptist red-
neck like my sons who often paddle through
the bluffs. But in a barn I placed a bed
and desk and dreamt the world. Gone from the coast,
I camp on hills of vanished Indians a few
calm nights and hear trees talk. I'm still a ghost.

Peddler and Tailor

My grandfathers come to me in an old film:
peddler and tailor going to the New World.
In the Old World the image blurs, unknown.
My bones, nose? I must be a bit like them.
Old photos say, look, here you were with a
black hat, white beard, dark faith in the one God.
But they stood dully in the light that day
in Lutz. They were despised. It wasn't odd
a century ago to flee. They wandered here
in steerage, climbing seven flights, and sat
in safety in their tenements. I hear
a plane, a wasp groaning under the sun.
Below I'm undespised and free: the son
peddling a soul and wearing no black hat.

The Good Beasts

On the first morning of the moon, in land
under the birds of Ur, before the flood
dirties the memory of a couple banned
from apples and the fatal fire of blood,
Adam and Eve walk in the ghetto park,
circling a tree. They do not know the way
to make their bodies shiver in the spark
of fusion, cannot read or talk, and they
know night and noon, but not the enduring night
of nights that has no noon. Adam and Eve,
good beasts, living the morning of the globe,
are blind, like us, to apocalypse. They probe
the sun, deathray, on the red tree. Its light
rages, illiterate, until they leave.

Eve, Paying for Truth, Drops Dead into the Eternity of Rain

Eve, who eats mainly fruit, tastes the bad end.
She is the first to go under the dark
and fade, but cannot feel surprise or spend
one micro-second to report the spark
of dull eternity burning her face
and liver like that wait before her birth.
She doesn't cringe or groan, but with the grace
learned from the flaming sword, exile on earth
and thorns of motherhood, she disappears
like an old lady curved over a mop
who quits her job and sinks. Eve has no fears
of light or loss of light and cannot know
the way. She isn't poor, and like a drop
of dust, merging with rain, begins to grow.

Buddha in the Twilight

Twilight. The Buddha smiles between the day
and dark. A million years of insects or
an ordinary fig tree shades the way
where Gautama sat down to think before
he organized a way to free the brain
of thought. He chose neither body nor god
but what is common to a star or grain
of earth or a Mongolian pony shod
with glittering iron: the atomic light
which each thing breathes inside. The Buddha smiles
and continents are vaguely false. His calm
obliterates a city. Before night
swallows the terror of non-being, he piles
a mountain in his hand. The empty palm.

210

Four Gospels of the Crucifixion

Joshua the Jew

King of the Jews, the soldiers name me, and
they spit, lay thorns upon me, smite my head,
while mocking and saluting. As the band
of Romans strips me, roughs me up—not dead
but rotting on Bad Friday—other men
dream up a way to warp the story of
my life on earth. Light of the world, but when
I use my balms to heal or speak of love
they lie and have me walking on the sea.
My simple arts they call a miracle.
I'm Joshua and a Jew. They change my name,
hating my blood, choking my identity
as rabbi. While I cry for help, my shame
is I am still a Jew, not God, they kill.

Yeshua the Gnostic

I, Yeshua, hanging on the cross
cry a bit, laugh because I know
only the man is aching. Loss
of blood is mystery as I grow
almost as green as sleep. But soon
I dream of Egypt, of the days
to tour. Good life. I was a friend
of boyhood when I saw the noon
turn midnight, when I felt the craze
to be a street magician and
to many till somehow I saw
the alien God. In my young hand
the eyes of heaven burn me. Raw
with light, I laugh up to the end.

Jesus the Christian

Saul the tentmaker spread the word: The Jew
the Romans killed was God. He came out of
the desert with a mustard seed that grew
into a mountain kingdom. Poised above
Jerusalem (the word means peace), he said:
I am the shepherd. Peace. Believe in me
and know the morning of the world. With bread
he fed a multitude, walked on the sea
in ghostly afternoon, and animals
out in the desert sighed. They crucified
the shepherd, who embraced the dark and died,
wine under earth. Then in his altered name
his Jews were killed, hunted and slain like whales
for oil, and he was God of death and shame.

Jesusa the Woman

Some say it is a man the Romans tacked
up on the cross. A man with naked breasts?
And that he screamed in pain when they attacked
him with a spear. I haven't screamed. Their jests
and insults pierced me more than labor on
the wooden beams. They lie about my sex,
yet you believe a gospel decades gone
after they spiked me up? And they perplex
me with their lofty souls, granting me slime.
I am a whore or witch or mother—not
a priest. Even the Pope cracked his Pole joke
saying I chose the apostles male. So choke
away up there. Millennia in the same spot.
I'm sick of rotting. Take me down. It's time.

Wang Wei and the Snow

Although Wang Wei is peaceful looking at
the apricot, the sea gull and the frost
climbing the village hills, or feels the mat
of pine trees on the mountain sky, or lost
in meditation loses nature and
the outer light to sing his way through mist
inside, although Wang Wei becomes the land
and loitering rain, his mountain clouds exist
as refugees from thought and turn like mills
never exhausting time. Wang Wei also
was stuck in life, and from his hermitage
he tells a friend to walk the idle hills
alone, to swallow failure like the age-
ing year, to dream (what else is there?) of snow.

Saint John Laughed on the Stairs

Saint John laughed on the stairs, a mystic child
with sun waking the wine. When cancer woke
his ulcerous skin, he chose to be reviled
in Úbeda. Nothing could paint the smoke
of his one-candle dark. In his black cell
he drank the science of his obscure love,
who came, who joined him and serenely fell
with him untellably. The black above
the earth was daybreak in his blood. Saint John
sat on the floor, babbled, and lived beyond
the word. Felicitous. The abscessed flesh
was nothing. 1591. A pond
of light. He drank the body of love, its fresh
illusion. Until death he lived with dawn.

Daydreaming of Anne Bradstreet and Her Eight Birds
Hatcht in One Nest

Anne Bradstreet and eight kids, your house burns down
near Ipswich, but with faith you bless the Lord
for each child he turns cold. Beasts cry concord
in the forests of New England, and each town
sings Sunday glory to white God. How far
we are this winter, Anne, domestic friend,
who can't know me or my three birds. I send
my admiration and a Christmas jar
of honey for your offspring (which you can't
accept, because of unresponsive time).
With all your books flaming in natural crime,
you sing of nakedness: an immigrant
to Heaven. I'm not reborn, but dream a plan
of forests, milk, and naked Mistress Anne.

Billy Budd

Billy knew how to make the ocean ring
with cloud-birds or the humming monsters in
the deep. The Handsome Sailor, mimicking
the illiterate nightingale, climbed up to win
his supper from the stars, and sang. He sang
tunes he made up to larger seafowl scream-
ing near the foretop. Barely a child of time,
from the maintop the angel had to hang,
for gagged by lies he had no words when quick
as flame from a night cannon his right arm
shot out and Claggart dropped. So through the mist
Billy ascended, and ascending took
the full rose of the dawn. Wordless his charm,
sleepy, now oozy weeds about him twist.

214

Chatting All Night with Dickinson in Her
New England Room

A light exists, your poems in which we talk
till dawn. You're in a white New England room,
I'm in a plane hanging like a nighthawk
outside. Though time is hungry germs, the doom
of friendship, doomsday now, wiping the past
away each instant, I will not submit
to losing you. You don't know me but last
night, each in our chair, we chatted, your wit
against the stranger. Wonder of the brain
that knows a window closed at death, yet keeps
a room after that room, after the chain
of dust, so we can speak alone. Your sleep
is false (or reader, even talk with you
is doomed), and Emily and I are snow.

Walt Foaming from the Mouth, 1892

Don't be surprised. I'm still hanging around,
talking to you. You thought me dead. I am
cheerfully in your room. I'm lost and found
and found and lost. A red-faced man, a ham,
and yet I'm laughing in the mountain air
out with my night bats floating. Don't be sick.
I failed. Emerson liked me, yet his care
cooled after one brave letter. Did he stick
by me? Why should he? Loudmouth, I contain
too much, embarrassing my friends. I shout
and whisper in your soul, and what you own
will rot, but not my words. When time speaks out
and death demands, do not go blank. The stain
of grass is deep. With me you're not alone.

Cavafy on His Own Bed above a Poor Taverna

The Jews and Christians of this city hound
me with their cults. "Despise those marble limbs
and worship the unseen." Bigots. They've found
an ally in Plotinos and their hymns
sing of a diamond heaven. It's no light
for my illicit afternoons whose sun
is candle weak, corrupt, and erudite
with kisses gambled on a strange bed. Son
of passion, I'm spent like burnt tobacco for
these nights of bloody thighs and lips. I use
a chaste demotic Greek and long ago
entombed my name in candid poems. I choose
the old city as my metaphor to know
rare limbs, old kings, and me, time's aging whore.

Antonio Machado in Soria, Jotting Lines
in a Copybook about Leonor Who Died

Walking in Old Castile, a widower
and young schoolmaster in my dirty clothes,
I'm gravely recreating Leonor
who left me in the spring. I almost loath
the adolescent fields, merino sheep,
blue peaks, the first whitening brambles, plums,
your child voice in my ear, yet walking numbs
intolerable whispers of the bed. To keep
your face, it's best to learn to wait. I will
know victory (or so the proverbs go)
and see an elm that lightning might ignite
and char. Dry elm a century on the hill,
still graced with leaves, my heart would also know
another miracle of spring and light.

Under the Colonels, I George Seferis on This Friday of Barbary Figs Say Hello to Blood

Two horses and a slow carriage outside
my window on the road in Spetsai where
I walk when everyone has gone to hide
under the cypress shade of sleep. The air
is salt, a gentle wind of brine and smells
from the old summer when a woman said,
"I am no sibyl, but your asphodels,
Antigone and blossoming seas are dead.
So let's make love." I am a diplomat
and poet, taste the archeologies
of old statues weighing me down, yet think
before I'm under house arrest I'll chat
and sleep with her. Help me, cut me. The sea's
live blood is better than a glass of ink.

God the Child

We are the same. Children. We both were born
in a dark sea, but I exist with warts
and wormy insomnia. God is a unicorn
chasing a mirror to destroy the quartz
precision of external time. I dream
a child's dream: both of us with sandwiches
and milk are wandering like an expert team
through cities of the pagans. Neither says
a word while blinded cows circle a well,
pulling up water. God tells me *he* made
the fields, the dust, the cows. I'm glad to know
someone like Einstein, warm and unafraid
to play with stars. Then back in time I grow
desolate. I made God who then made hell.

God in the Bathroom Mirror

Though I lay nine months sharing blood and food,
curled in my mother's sack, I quake alone,
and since my birth I've breathed in solitude.
In solitude I come on love and loan
my heart, wounded in solitude by love,
seeking oblivion, union, and the peace
of being found and lost, with logic of
a head drunk in transcendence or hot seas
of blood. God is my choice, though he is me.
I am a fool before my powers to fool
the mind, and weak before such ecstasy
of hope. Flat on the bathroom rug I scratch,
edgy while vapory God burns on the glass,
in solitude: a steamy, ticking jewel.

The Watchmaker God

You save perfection for yourself. We are
the movements running down, the crooked wheel,
while you the maker are the awful star
in harmony with nothing wrong. I feel
insulted by your absence. Yet, if you
were real, I'd be diminished. I am I
alone in my glass world. I hurt, I cry
(humiliating act) and can't get through
with words. I fail repeatedly and lose
the face I love. The hands fall off! Just time
to shout. I hate your secret life and cruise
against a cosmic glass. I'd rather be
a mumbling imbecile than a dumb mime
of your perfection. I am spooked and free.

God the Miser of Time

I do not love you, God. If you have ears,
record it: old mafioso bishop, lack-
ing decency, your power enlarged by fears,
dumb to compassion, deaf to justice, black
at night when darkness hangs on us, and white
against the sun, but never seen out there
or in the mind. You said "Let there be light"
and there was darkness, chaos everywhere.
Words and no voice. I do not love you, Lord,
for you, miser of time, do not love me,
never give back one look or holy word.
You'll never be, although I rant absurd-
ly to the graceless ghost. Αξιον εστι[1]
the death in which I am already poured.

God Our Light

Like obscure poets in a Midwest town
whose voice will never reach the world, or in
the Zaïre courtroom where the judge puts down
his gavel, ordering death, and all eleven
young officer defendants jerk erect-
ly to their feet and then are shot that day,
their intellectual voices hushed, dissect-
ed from their hearts by fire, their obscure way
to fame some lead marks in the *Times*, so all
of us act out obscurely, with a flare
at times, a life alone, disguised by love
and every public act, before we fall
into the absolute ditch, seen from above
only by God—our light—who's never there.

---

[1] Worthy be

God on Trial at Auschwitz

I go to God by slipping dimly crazed,
dropping through graves, and not a dream, and wake
from day, felicitous, roaring, amazed
by light. The Lord is lurking as the snake
of heaven and I know that death when all
surprise of solitude is gone. Some sheep
wobble on a blue meadow, on the tall
sunny blue Mosque where God has gone to sleep
it off, snoring, dazzling, and high. I see
his throne and chariot, parrot and the stars
consuming dream. But in his bed our God
is put on trial at Auschwitz. Now the scars
of tattooed numbers kill my ecstasy.
I bump lonely against the holy fraud.

The Stranger in Southern Indiana

I must go. Not home. I live in an oak barn
in the woods. What better dream? The glass wall
lets sun or the full moon like a ghost fall
on a blue Bukhara or a chair with yarn
and books. No chair of joy. Outside, in town
the teams, opera and friends are all remote.
I care for them. Only I don't like me float-
ing where there is no ocean. I slip down,
a dry ghost among ghosts. Where can I go?
Athens, Maine, NY? Roots? I'm everywhere,
and having no intimate love or face
to study, I've gone, yes, somehow I'm there
already in those woods where I efface
this strangeness. Where? I'm dead and cannot know.

The Coffee House

Others are here for talk. I've come to find
salvation, so the coffee hardly trims
my arrogance. Sadly I suck the mind
of grounds for hints of grace. The napkin swims
bloated on hot tea spilled across the table
into my lap, burning me. The quick fix
of feeling, but I hold out for an angel
to float through caffeine vapor on its six
luminous wings. The waitress, circling by
the edge of purgatory, asks me what
I want. (To know the Book of Eve, I think,
or peel an onion down to its gray sky
of peace.) "A cappuccino, please." I shut
my heart and watch the coffee turn to ink.

Christmas Day

The snow crisscrosses down and flurries up
all afternoon, unaware it is snow
or some of us are desperate, or the radio
(unaware too) has Mimi drink a cup
of wine on Christmas eve. I work alone
in this dead building. Sons are sleeping. They
have thirty years before the middle way
of hell's dark forest. Don't give up. My own
nowhereness please forget. I go downstairs
for yogurt, smash the vender with my shoe
(it gypped me). *Buona sera, Mimi.* I'm through
with gray Bohemia. Resolute I stare
at junk and snow, and take a photo of
my heart, guessing at speed, focus and love.

Coffee in Predawn Buenos Aires

Depression is a sickness of the lips,
for words don't vibrate. Sleep hangs on the will
like months of blackness on Cape North, and grips
the pocket of the heart, squeezing, until
mere sleep is a food riot. But I don't climb
the walls. I'm low, not a mad bug. The wall
is an underworld city fog. Café time
before the dawn is for a hermit. All
the global light is out. I sip my blue
coffee mug, nursing the cool slop. The phone
and morning crowds uplift me from the slough
of solitary vision. When they're gone
I'm back in me, hanging in fog. Despair
and underworld I've earned as moles earn prayer.

A Rose in Hell

After slopping through hell along three roads,
I stumble on a rose. Insane? A flower
in this dark land where we hop dark like toads
in darkness. Beasts. I hear Moscow's red hour
of revolt. No. I am too tired, too old
not to reform. Too much bathos of hell.
My tape plays old French songs. White rose. A bell
wakes the grand organ of the Tzar. I've sold
my house, bought an exhilaration shoe
to walk beyond the Caucasus. I try,
goodbye. I'm really well, and will fall on
a resurrection. Don't tell me I lie.
Can't I get out? I'm almost tunneling through
to ice, a secret rose, and blizzard dawn.

Spirit Has a Beginning

Although there's no Director of the Scenes
working especially for me, I bet
what happens is for good. Forgot my jeans
in Hong Kong; on a marble hill in Crete
I left a lens. Yesterday in Nepal
a boy got my glasses. Why do I lose
my things? Alms to the cosmos? When I fall
in love, it lasts a life, but I confuse
my lover, lose her, and walk for years
on fire. It's good. Rain will surprise my heart
one day before I die. Theologies
despise possessions, and I feel no tears
for things—though lost love replays death. Yet these
words come because I lose. Loss is a start.

Sun

Sun is the eye. Out there. A glaring, black,
impossible-to-look-at fire. It creeps
on insects, under water, in the crack
of falcon cliffs, on fuzzy eggs. It sleeps
on beads of planets strung on cosmic rings.
Its hydrogen explosions warm the flute
of rays poking through moonclouds, and its wings
of morning celebrate the garden fruit
with hymns of life. On gum and cinnamon
and every spice it heats the chlorophyll.
When Galileo looked through flaming glass
he told the truth and burned. Its miracle
alone makes light, the eye inside, a gas
of yellow worlds, the dark night of the sun.

Reindeer

One night in Lapland I was in the street
with a young nun who held me in her arms.
The sun was weird and strong, washing our feet
with northern rays. We wandered to the farms
outside of town. She was a socialist
and French—so delicate. Two winters in
a sardine factory. When our spirits kissed
I blessed la Petite Soeur, feeling her chin
against my neck. Our union was a stain
of hope for both of us. I cashed a check
at Olaf Bull's and spent another week
with her among the fjords where houses were
uncommon dreams like us. We were insane-
ly stubborn, free—real reindeer in that blur.

Song of the Birds

After Pablo Casals had taped the Song
of the Birds, high on Canigo, we went
by foot, from the old French convent, along
the mountain rug of stars, down to the scent
of wheat. We couldn't see. You held my hand
because the trail was steep. Then in the grove
we saw ourselves. Naked. By the command
of natural soul, we lay down young and drove
our blood. Our tongues were water, our eyes huge,
earth an unknowing fire until the dawn
of cows and village children screaming led
us back. I loved you in our pure refuge
against the law. The night was sun. Though gone,
our virgin mountain is a lucent thread.

Happiness of the Patient Traveler

I wrote a letter to the sun
to shine on us again for one
more life. Then begged him for the time
to let our tongues agree to rhyme
for one more year. And then I asked
for just a day, but he unmasked
me with the alphabet of night,
and when I pleaded for more light
he spat on me with hours of rain
which finally washed away the pain
of time. I wrote a letter to
the sun and said I would let go
of love. He led me to a tree
inside, where I could hang and be.

The Black Hill

There are two ways to fail. (And failure is
the providence we come to when in time
we tumble out of consciousness to mis-
erable extinction.) One way is to climb
inside. The hill is black on a plateau
where iron moondogs screech like cables. Light
can't understand that darkness, yet black snow
thinks, spreads like thunder where I saw a white
heaven of calm seconds. The other way
climbs out to you, gambling on bliss, begins
with a look, words, and our huge walk above
the city. We are drifting gulls, two pins
through a slow century. I choose the love
out there. Help me. To make the black hill day.

Sirens

Sirens are singing monsters of the sea
who live on mountains in the north. A bridge
connects two peaks, and from that height I see
their yellow eyes: star beacons on the ridge,
longing to shake me into the abyss.
Their passion fills my ears. I've thrown away
the wax, and despite trembling cowardice
I hear the river in their throats. My way
is clear. Their fatal weapon is my choice.
The singing pierces the protective fan
of lead under my clothes. Their wings explode
like virtue cracking through a Puritan.
Easy as consciousness, I jump, a toad
into the waters of their cloudy voice.

Archaic Faces on the Wall

On Saturday the judge will tell me: "Go
to freedom." (Santorini once was green
like glassy pitchers, but the lava flow
scorched and froze the island in an unseen
time trap where the hill castle's chalky steps
circle down to the port.) The day before
the legal end, I say: "Come, any place,
even a city room for rent. We'll soar
windy like gulls. Alive." And yet no call
or easy babbling talk. Daydream? I kid
myself. Ancient terror of freedom. Again
the knife of freedom paints me on the wall
next to a tender face. Terror amid
the mouths—ours—poised and begging oxygen.

Into the Meadow of Absence

I see. Am not the vision. Where I am
is not the body living in a hut
in Cold Mountain pine groves, or one that swam
near Sodom in the bromine slime that cut
its thighs and burned its vision to the cry
of Samson's noon. I'm not that dark, that rare
high Asian solitude or alibi
of body plotting with the photosphere
for rapture in the ultraviolet air!
Secretly now, I've come into the clear
meadow of absence, to the dumbfound shade
of being behind the eyes, the punctured dream
of sun outside. Perfect, in terror, I seem
to be. But where I look all bodies fade.

A Guy Eating Tomato Salad by the Grape-Eternal Sea

A table on an island. And a man
with his tomato salad, overhear-
ing screams inside the smoky kitchen. An
eternal grape sea burns around his sphere
of longing for the wheat between her thighs,
for cherry nipples flagrant in beach sun,
that naked woman with a flute, laugh, eyes
hiding the pumice cave. For him a nun
moon-bellied of remote mad blood. And so
he pounds Cyclopean walls and then forgets
what talking is, lies like red ants below
the blue air trapping him to obscure birth
on the floor. I'm in him. And when he sweats
I'm near his skin, scheming to be the earth.

Apollo in Náxos

Huge kouros on its back and not alive,
not even finished, but the eyes are blur
of mountains behind mountains under five
layers of mist; the huge lips are a slur
of rocky lust, never to kiss or talk.
Life as stone is simple: the mammoth arm
intense yet calm in the gold marble lock
of time. I'm never still and seldom calm
and feel a fly's six twitching legs. The dark
profiles of mountains of the night are never
enough to burn a way of gold, a spark
of cosmic life. The soul is soul, stone stone.
The kouros stares into the air forever,
a phantom of live rock. We're each alone.

Cyclops in Sérifos

Cyclops looks up to fire. The sun returns
his gaze, and figs, sea, wild carnations glow
under its wings of dawn! The monster spurns
reflection. Born of words, he doesn't know
the will of time wasting the wildest thighs,
the myth of death which only haunts the blood
of meditative creatures. Though time lies
in space, rotting the giant's ponderous food
and butchered eye, my thought secretly gives
a life to Cyclops. Why should vulgate sun
constrict my dream or time erode the myth
of groping Cyclops? Time will blur us with
its wing of night (we are its fugitives).
The light in us is all of time. Then gone.

Staying Up Late in a Big Empty House in Hamilton, N.Y., Where Rain Comes Late to Keep Me Company

About three every morning like a mole
I move with glass eyes, dreaming up a path
of light, stumbling with hot milk toward the bath
where futilely I finger glass. No soul
floats on the mirror. Souls don't come with eyes,
but the insomniac sees just her green face.
Rain starts to chew the roof and unifies
the forest. Sound of plankton in the mouth
of whales. Rain. Rain. And suddenly the moss
of darkness clears to a blue pearl! The light
invented, while I sit on dirty clothes,
concocting dream. In blurry indecision
I climb in bed and fall like rain from sight
where neither soul nor glasses fix my vision.

The Panther

The panther has no mission but her night
of milk and moon. I float from bed. Pad down
into the room where lemons are the light
of asteroids, hungry in the sepia brown
and melancholy space, the basement where
like birth I start. The blood outside is clouds;
inside my chest the gold forest of hair
grows out of beads of grease. These are the shrouds
around the ruby. Wondrously she came:
a voice. Violet night is honey. I break
the easy lock and follow the command
of the moonwind, far lake of fire, the hand,
roar, the dark ruby panther! Only flame
of her dark heart sings, sings. I live to wake.

The Lamp

The lamp is everywhere, lighting the stag,
the lily and the sons and daughter of
the paper sun, the ink greening the rage
of memory. Of course the lamp is love.
But how to wake? Love is invented shad-
ow of a shadow. Wasps and worms. At night,
weak vision, but the lamp creates the mad
and reasoned rose, its lips in which the light
folds deep as Africa, black as the globe.
I own one body and a mortal soul
in whom the eye is a dead moon, a hole
of dust, the wake of flame. The orphan Job
called for the Lord. I call for fire, wait long
for fire, to see the rose open in song.

On the Floor of the Creation

I wait. Is there a second when we do
not wait? Quevedo made a man so thin
he was a fork, with rats housed in one shoe,
roaches rooming in the other. Yet in
his heart already yellowing like teeth,
he dreamt of shining at the court. We wait
(in Romance it means *hope*) but underneath
the coming (never here) of desolate
and flaming death is the sad going (never gone)
of every second since the flood at Ur.
I pull the shade. Sun. Suddenly the damp
Midwest is Babylon. I'm on the floor
of the Creation, under a clay lamp,
a child, captive to hope, scheming at dawn.

Gospel of Clouds

On cloudy Sundays clouds are in my heart
as if my brother came, as if the rain
lingered among the mushrooms and the art
of freedom washed into the murder train
or rinsed the peat bog soldiers of the camp.
On cloudy Sundays clouds are with Joe Hill
(last night I dreamt he was alive); the tramp
was mining clouds for thunder. And uphill
into the clouds I feel that time descends,
as if my mother came, as if the moon
were flowering between the thighs of friends
and gave us fire. On Sundays when the swan
of death circles my heart, the cloudy noon
rolls me gaping like dice, though I am gone.

Yellow Cottage

The yellow cottage in the woods is sun
among the cherry trees, a clapboard glass
on which the father fire becomes a fawn
startled in August. Hands of uncut grass
finger the windows' black abandonment.
Mr. Ketcham the drunk, dead on the floor,
was dropped wet in the earth of white Vermont
and in the dark ferments. But is there more?
A soul? Or hope of secret space? Was he
translated to the chamber of the stars,
the crystal cottage where the fire and dew
of heaven feed the farmer? Two old cars
are rotting in the weeds. Mr. Ketcham's tree
of life is dreamless, still, and earthly blue.

Quaker Love

The Shakers, who died out for lack of love
in sheets, made beds and chairs erect and plain,
and Friday nights they shook the rafters of
their hall with song and danced away the pain
of stark abstention. With a Quaker crew
I go to Mexico to dig some holes
and nail some wooden seats to shit into
so Zapotecs can squat and learn our roles
of hygiene. Then I quake with you. To see,
to hear, to touch, to kiss, to die with thee
in wildest sympathy! Turn off the light.
Bodies are all we are. After still night
comes birth, some light, the vast forgetting and
the blows of love. Sleep, sleep and hold my hand.

If I Could Phone the Soul

The night is beautiful. I live alone
and hope. It's better than to be the king
of rainy nations. Yet if I could phone
the soul, my soul, your soul, or see my being,
if I could sleep outside of time a while
and know why I am ticking toward a sleep
where time will fail (at least for me), I'd smile.
I smile right now, which means I groan, I creep
with shame because I'll always be a fool.
The night is beautiful. I pray. I lie.
I love. I'm happy. Everyone is poor,
especially the king of rain whose rule
drops me dead on a moon where I can't die.
I'm stupid. Love is you. We have no cure.

Vagrants

The sad are lucky for they feel and know
they have a being, because it aches. The loss
of love is common malady. I go
shabbily to a loft, and ring. Friends toss
a key in a white sock down from the sky.
Climbing the warehouse stairs, I smell the cat-
piss in the trash and feel the rain or sigh
of rags and vagrants in Penn Station at
the phone booths. I am desolate not sick
(for age has not yet rammed its plumber's snake
into a heart of deathbed wisdom), yet
the rays of lofty sun and women prick
my heart. Climbing endlessly high, upset
by peace, I drown unsweetly in its lake.

Gospel of Lies

Comrade illusion, I embrace you like
a tuba. Gold and false. My hero Don
Quijote rose up mad and set his pike
against the gales of mills and monsters on
the wasteland of La Mancha. Jesus al-
so toured, performing magic, and he gave
his life so we might drink the alcohol
of heaven, drink the light and be no slave
of truth. Even the Buddha found a way
to free the unsubstantial self and fly
inside a dream of sun. Until the sun
was gone Quijano lived the noble lie
of lunacy: the poor man with a day
of grace and fire. Then true oblivion.

Gospel of the Tower

Back in the tower (scheming a way out of
the tower) I drink a coke to heal my sad-
ness while the opium rain is washing love
out of the heartland night. But it's not bad
alone with books. A lover eats the soul
exquisitely, yet I chew books and hear
my worries sing in the amazing hole
of *nous* amid my flesh, an airy sphere
with ozone gaps. I am with books which do
not judge or hate me, an astronomy
of ink I love and ponder while below
the janitors are playing cards. I play
with letters like Jehovah at the Tree:
vain, lonely maker reading till the day.

A Car Ferry in Northern Vermont

The car's up front. Overhead, gossipy birds
worry about the ferry in the sun.
Destiny east. I've spent my life on words
although below the sea the words are gone.
Slowly the talk, friends, love born on a hill
become a haze of gulls. Way back. The sky
below the sea was closed even to Gil-
games who couldn't undo death. To die
is nature, but the boat is ticking on
into the sun. It's WHITE out there. Sun white!
and our few hours elect eternity
until we dock down in the carless night
below. I sigh for love lost in the sea
although below the sea the dark is gone.

Snow and Woods

Tonight I'm sad with ink. It's coming. Spring.
Yet since I sleep curled in a smile, why care
about the voice of thirty years? I sing
off-key in my own garden. Sun meets air,
heats it gently. I ask for one gold coin.
Not more. A gull comes with the sun. My peace
is warm, yet pain under the mind again
stands by my chair. In years of roaming Greece
I loved white walls on cypress fields, and here
I smell the memory of spring. The night
is blue with brandy; love like snow around
the house glares with remorse and open fear.
The snow is hot, and woods are filled with light,
for the sad spring or love moves in the ground.

Gospel of the Mountain

On a red mountain north of Beijing (where
the Chinese hermits banished morning frost
by chopping wood), the wisdom of the air
washes the silent herons. Time is lost
like a smoke wisp hanging over bamboo.
Time of no-mind. The mountain cherries bloom
by the white hut, and life is never through
although the heart can never leave its room.
One life, caught on the planet, never with
the burning spice of immortality.
On a red mountain, mist and sunlight hold
some peaceful lemon trees in their own myth
of joy. The long disease of history
is far off screams. The lemon air is cold.

Gospel of Light

The moon is natural in the evening. I
cannot be angry at it. And a flute
high on the mountain is the sweetest lie
of separation. And the stench of fruit,
fogging the blasted lots, over the quake
in the Algerian city, joins the dead
who don't smell sweet. Yet in the inner lake
of light, *lake of the heart* as Dante said,
the rays are stronger than the suffering
and rapture of the outer world. To be
inside and be the light is everything
I want. For now I live seized by the wall,
those ten walls of the flesh, and what I see
is glaring dark, that is, nothing at all.

Gospel of the Night

Plotinos sang the way to lose the way
outside. His Alexandria blurs. The streets
become illusion. As he fades, a ray
of darkness fills the wilderness and heats
the night with ecstasy. The ONE above
the night, the sun who never can be seen
(the seer is the seen) is all and love
and joy connecting atoms. Yet between
the flight of the alone to the alone,
the climb, the circling up to light, I've been
a creature of the streets, and I suspect
you share my vagrant sadness. If we groan
the clouds are safely in the clouds. Abject-
ly dark, I thank the night for raining in.

Mandolin

Bring me a mandolin. Let it be Greek
as my life is when I am floating high
with pain or passion, pausing on the peak
that is the noon of night and love. I sigh
with you, we speak at the white corner of
the mountain village, we are wise, we see
too well. Magic is live. Don't look above
for miracle. Magic is here, a tree
like the white olive in our heart. Though death
is not a way to miracle, is dread
dimming our being, senseless, out of our skin,
with age I float outside. You float. Your breath
is mine. We're many. Just a lip or bed
or phone away. Bring me a mandolin.

Pearl

The universe is ticking, and the pearl
(hidden from day down in the ocean floor)
burns in its shells. And though the watery pearl
is small, its eye is a transparent core
deep as the macrovoid and everywhere.
Leviathan of light ticking in the sea
in buried shells. To know it! And lose care,
hunger, because the milk in every tree,
white sap in every mountain, the moon bulls
pinning the sky of ice in place
all feed on it. In ignorance we feed
on the electrons of the pearl, its face
of plenitude. For just one poisoned bead
of opal fire we dive and gorge like gulls.

Gospel of Time

The wheels of an invisible timepiece
are whirring someplace in the mind, almost
as fine as quartz. Einstein knew the peace
outside where lines become a single ghost
embracing at infinity, but in
the living head there is no end to planes
or time. I feel that clock. It says *Ich bin*
like Rilke's silent friend turning the pains
of living into wine or transformation,
and in the mammoth night a blatant cock
of dawn cannot intrude. The almond tree
weeps amber yet, like us, feels no creation
or death (that's just for others). But my clock
knows one, outrageous, final mystery.

Gospel of Snow

Death is an insult, since it proves I am
only a witness of a solitude
and you're asleep. I am just one mad clam
pushed by infinite seas and slurped as food
by time. You dream. I feel the planet spin
like a big lettuce in a flooding sink.
Then floating with the vegetables, I'm in
this time bomb skinbag: hairy, lusty, pink.
To be just me is bad enough! To go
and be no more is unforgivable.
Why not be cheerful like my dog's green eye?
He's fixed but smart and loves me. When you sigh,
lemon trees blossom in your heart. It's all
we have—a bit of love, some fire. And snow.

Imaginary Beings

The ghosts are you I live with on a ship
of snow. I'm dreaming on my cabin bed,
over the hold of worms, and taste the lip
of lunacy. And "Love," Machado said,
"is in the absence," so your arms of light
tickle my watch. You are invisible
as are the gulls around the moon, or night
horizons blond like Easter bread. You still
the singing whales. You smell of fire. Sick of
accusing faces down in the iron mess
of this black ship, weary of the jaguar
or shark or iron bureaucrat of love,
I love your ghostly words, your clouds, your star
of snow, your laughter at my loneliness.

Room

Returning to my room—it has my lamp,
some shirts, a photo of my daughter, and
a second pair of shoes—I am a tramp
among the worthy (I think proudly). Banned
like Mandelstam, grave as Celan, I feed
my night with firebirds and the postcards found
with poems in a dead man's trench coat. Greed
for fame is infamous. Do I confound
the word with me? The *me*—well, trivial
and often taken for the word—has its
own grievance with salvation's clock. But in
my room where even stars circle in jail,
poems were born in faith and lucky fits.
I'm lucky! Now a shirt to hide my skin.

Singer

They call me solitude they call me by
the name of my disgrace the child and so
I'm drunk on corners of the sky and shy
although the moon painted the street with snow
so don't abandon me in the white night
I leave the city looking for my child
who is like me crazy and kiss the light
of sister planets the police are mild
with me a harmless nut O serene friend
under the jasmine air you are like me
guilty of heat of feeling trees of salt
or opals in the mouth what agony
of freedom they won't shoot us it's my fault
for singing child I love you we offend.

Gospel of Love

We took our cycle to the lovers' cliff
at Ronda where the knights murdered a bull
or fought the Moors. Sore from the road and stiff,
we sat where Rilke (in the fanciful
old Quaker lady's inn) sat by the fire,
hearing the verse of Góngora the Jew.
It seems a century ago: desire
for sun, refinement, and for white and blue
Sevilla, oranges, and the Spring Fair,
five nights of dancing into dawn. Sunday
morning in fascist Spain, the women rode
their flowery stallions. Salt was in the air
as we cycled on the coast. That episode
of wonder was our childhood sun. Our way.

Inlight

Through the mind's window and its black horizon
the inner eye descends to feeble sun
flickering like the last *Kyrie eleison*
in a Greek dome outside. Oblivion
of sun drifts between fires like a patient
circling near death. The candle flares and just
a flicker. No one knows the last descent
into the chest of night where time is dust
everywhere. And inlight? Does it have waves
or particles? Its luminosity
hangs from the spirit. Flick, it's gone. And while
alive it hides. It means itself. To be
the light; to stand inside the sun and smile,
loving the sun. Until the night, it saves.

Gospel of Fire

In this red room of Paris student days,
under the bulb drooping over the hull
of a wood cot, my novel floods with word plays
of sex and existential thieves. I pull
the window down—a cement patio where
a Dutch blonde rooms, who once looked up at me
with young misery as if she felt the stare
of my desire. I read on. No way to be
with her. On the wall right behind my bed,
wallpaper smiling lewd with its black teeth
begins a Quaker shake. I hear the flow
of a loud mattress, light a match beneath
my hand (I'm smoking pipes), and Heer Van Gogh
watches my fingers flaming on the bed.

Gospel of Failure

Raining a week, so all the clouds doze on
the poisoned fields, yet now the sun intrudes,
toweling the rainy light. The Parthenon
is still afloat, and underground old nudes
of marble wait for some new sewer dig to
restore their time. I row below the stars
of roaring silences while in Chengdu
some acrobats, poor devils full of scars,
go at each other, slapping swords and fire
against their bodies. As I sit and row
on my machine, my poems collapse below
fat time's rejection. Work, love, being; desire
for more than death. Flopping I laugh. Dogs hear
me fart, bark from the basement at my fear.

Secret Criminal

There's no one I can trust. I do have friends.
Confess to them? And make it three times worse,
trying to prove my crimes have noble ends?
I'm not a happy spy mingling a purse
with patriotism. Sleep is theirs, not mine.
Back in Damascus as I climb each stair
up to her room, it is a hidden mine
field where the slightest noise will strip me bare
and get me shot. I have a knife. I never
reach back for it. Once in the jumbled bed
I use my charm, I lie with truths to sever
the muezzin's predawn moaning from my talk.
I enter her. She moans. She cries. She's dead.
Outside, I walk. No one to tell. I walk.

242

Gospel of the Executed

Horace Dunkins, Jr., died in the chair,
early Friday after the second try.
His uncle and his father stayed their prayer
nineteen minutes for the Alabama eye
of justice to discover and repair
the faulty hookup of electrodes by
replugging cables in. With volts to spare
the executioner flipped the green switch
and the mildly retarded killer, still
unconscious, breathing, died without a hitch,
the first to taste the federal gift to die.
Our Supreme Court ruled that the state could kill
Dunkins. By voting five to four to slay
retards (and children too), they cleared the way.

Arnost Lustig Listens to the Sound of People Being Shot

Snow coming down is mingling with the ash-
smoke from the crematorium's nearby stack.
I feel the silence and barbed wire, the rash
of shots, the urge to run out into black-
ness and put my dead lips under the snow.
In just fifty-four days three hundred thousand
of Warsaw's Jews are rounded up and go
to the gas chambers in Treblinka. Frau and
Herr Toten dance all night. The people fall
into their absence. Snow on faces when
they hit the ground. The barracks lends obscene
witness to my depravity. Hear all
those faces drop into snow. Please listen
to bleakness. Time is dying. We're unseen.

Homeless with AIDS

John of the Cross, the mystic, lived to be
inside and burn, to climb through darkness up
to light and die from time in ecstasy
of union and oblivion. His cup
of love he gave to his erotic God.
The youth of China and the Argentine
also kissed death with passion, wasted blood,
dying for nation. Caught in my benign
and tiny hole of air, I'm weak. It shames
me empty. On a New York corner where
a young and downcast guy sits by his sign
and cup HOMELESS WITH AIDS, as I go near
I look away, yet toss a buck. It tames
me. "Thanks a lot, brotha" stings in my ear.

Baudelaire and His Parisian Dead

Am I perverse through your pain, Baudelaire,
your dead, your poor Parisian dead so cold
and skeletal, forgotten in the prayer
of worms where no friend, no Lord, comes to hold
their rotting hearts so they can fly above
the scum of earth up to a cottage white
and beautiful where ice cannot kill love,
where blood nostalgia leaks a dream of light,
where black John Henry finally rose and slept
and all our misery is grace? Am I
perverse to drink your pain? I'm happy since
we are the same—we're lost, we wake to die,
and when death comes at least our ignorance
will help us feel, to feel and not accept.

Homeless

Pascal has his abyss inside, and Baudelaire
walks in the twilight streets with the clochards
through dingy Paris while the hungry stare
across the empty Seine; dull drunkards spar
with cold, and beggar women with a can
of fire blow on the burning sticks to warm
their hands and sagging breasts. Worst is the dawn
when the Hotels of God extend an arm
to draw the dying to a Catholic bed
of hope. While Pascal tramps the sores and blaze
of hell and Baudelaire in decadence
pities the damned like him, the homeless dead
smell bad in New York doorways. Yet when haze
burns off, their souls leak out in innocence.

Return from the Snow

My father in the nineteenth century
was born in Boston, tragic, on Milk Street.
My mother was a Maineiac like me
from Marsden Hartley's town. Death went to meet
them young. They only knew me young,
will never see my photo turning gray
nor have a clue about my life among
the Greeks. I'd like to walk their shoes away,
crossing this holy island. Life is like
the wind: it blows a while out of the east
with sun and grapes; as soon as it is felt
it blows again with ice. I feel the spike
of thorns along the rocky meadows melt
with love as they walk with me to our feast.

Grykos, Patmos

Mary's Version

The Christians stole my life. I was a Jew,
an unembellished wife and mother till
the Romans pounded nails in Josh. It's true
he coughed up magic parables—but kill
a guy for that? Then Matt, Mark, Luke and John
gossiped with visionaries, dreamt up tales,
made me unreal and cast him as a con-
man, yes, a stuntman popping miracles
to fool the world. Their curve on history
was holy gospel lies and my despair.
The facts: I never went to rallies in
the fields, Josh wasn't God, I had my spin
with Joe, and Joshua was our son. I swear
there is no bastard in my family tree.

My Daughter Heads Me to Felicity

When the bad hour of climbing to the roof
to float like Father from the sun is lurking,
however stupidly in mind, the proof
of happiness is sound, for what is working
deep in the cave is love. My daughter tells
me wisely that the hour of happiness
is here, and I agree. And then she spells
it out, insisting that I not repress
the pain. Cry, if you can. Though I'm ashamed
of weakness and my sad and groveling plea
for love, she wakes me free. I'm free. She's right,
of course. I love her truth: not to be named
by Adam, live or dead. And in my night
like sun I float in strange felicity.

Tramping around Beijing

A night in Beijing as I tramp the street
of snow and mule aromas to my room,
a flute hangs on the cabbage mounds. I eat
a moon cake while the all-night factories fume
with blue fluorescent tubes and drudgery
of progress. But the flute persists. It climbs
with Buddhist pause, soaring to the fire tree
of goldfish stars. Out there no words or rhymes
are heard. How strange! when here I am the fool
again, learning a tongue, and cocked to damn
my pen to bliss, to the good news of verse,
to gospel song. Of course alone. The rule
of silence, Chinese vast, is fixed. I nurse
that faith of silence. Yet, please hear: I am.

Soul Light

The soul is light, her body living mud.
And although soul light is invisible,
once gone her lonely ark fades in the flood
of death, angelfish glare, the bleaching gill
is stiff to bubbling air, the clam is tight
around her shrinking cloud of fat. So take
me now. Make my mud bake, crack in the light
of light! I ask for little. Help me wake
and be my friend. I love you, yes. The soul
is a small gift of the creation. For
one yellow night of love, the butcher shop
soaks lilies in her blood. Soon I will drop:
a black varicose watch into the floor
of time. I love you from my shining hole.

Ophelia the Singer

Ophelia sang as she was drowning in
the brook, and snatches of old tunes were heard
above the glassy stream while her warm skin,
in garments weighted with her madness, blurred
and sank her melody to muddy death.
Her lay was drowned yet heard by all who sing
and choose—incapable of noise on earth—
to end the fantasy of transient being.
Among the daisy fires of their distress,
they try to sing. I saw my father croon,
I heard my brother dream. You'll stick it out
since every second's better than the dress
of darkness. Kick me, sing me, toss me, soon
like a plug nickel I'll be back and shout.

Overlooking Rock Meadows of Forbidden Albania

That night it rained a thousand years and when
my heart was soaked, Mólista windows turned
to sleet. The cold intensified. Again
between your breasts I read you poems we earned
in Greek because this mountain cottage near
the Albanian border was a single lamp
and moon-coarse blankets smelled of wool winter
and candles. "Don't expect to sleep." Souls damp
with longing blare like sirens. We were still
because we had the speech of solitude.
A thousand years is nothing for a pound
of rain together. We made love. To fill
the soul with bread and olive oil is crude
and wonderful. Night gossiped while we

Franz Kafka in His Small Room on the Street of the Alchemists, 1916-1917

One winter Kafka rented a white room
high near the castle where he tired his pen
during the day. At night he rinsed the gloom
out of his eyes and was a crow in heaven,
rising, dancing on awful heights. Before
dawn fed him sleep, the Golem far below
the wall whispered a gravesong in his ear
in ancient Hebrew vague to him. Although
he slept, the ghost of Jewish friends in Prague
(Max Brod who loved his ink) helped him
survive close to the sky. A winter wood
of horses floated on the city fog.
The castle mastered him, but in a whim
he drank white ink and hungered where he stood.

Love Bade Me Welcome

"I loath the mindless, ticking universe,"
Love said to me. "Gross stars roll through the dark
and time performs. But once gone through the verse
of life, no time will pulsate in your art-
less death. So talk to me and don't abstain."
Love took my hand. "I'm all you have," she said.
"You must sit down," she begged me. "I'll not chain
you to a bed." I stuttered and my bread
got stale. "Forget my soul and taste my meat,"
Love urged. But I withdrew to pout (Would sin
prevail?). Stars hurl and burn. Afraid she'd slip
into my sheets and rage my frozen skin
with joy, I turned to flee and saw a ship.
Love sighed, "Before you drown, sit down and eat."

With a French Nun in Lapland

Even the constant sun wears a small coat
of darkness till it bangs into our light.
A nun in Lapland on a ferry boat,
whose lips are frozen God, whose hood is white
with ice floating the fjords, unzips my pants
to show her grace. "I'll keep this memory,"
she whispers, "in my bones and sardine cans
back in the factory where I share my tea
and labor with the workers." Sun hangs on
all night in Lapland in July. I bless
my friend the nun for sun. A socialist
and French she talked to clouds over our fun
and deer licks. When our bellies join, no less
than mountains blush and crush us in their fist.

A Sunny Room at Mount Sinai

Mount Sinai Hospital. My mother lay
in a good corner room with lots of sun.
In Perigueux, the children's ward, one day
I saw a young girl in a coma. Sun
came through glass walls; the child was beautiful,
her face freshened with youth. Only inside
the cancer stormed. I saw the nun place wool
soaked in cold alcohol on her. She died
that afternoon. My mother's gown was loose
and she told us that awful things were done
when testing her downstairs. I see her eyes
today. She too was fresh and live. Some juice
lay undrunk by her pillow. A surprise
of pain. I left the room and she was gone.

A Roof Bed in Mexico

Last Sunday the new boarding house smelled good.
Popo was clear. Even its volcanic smoke looked clean
from my roof bed that faced the serpent plains where Cortés
    stood
shining like the dread white god Quetzalcuatl seen
as God prophetically returning to break the Aztecs there
by the temples at Cholula. We bussed across
that llano and down the carnation mountains to the coast.
    Vera Cruz was a huapango fair
of masks and trumpets and we danced. Then loss
of virginity. What loss? We woke
and entered rooms of love, our lives. Back in the city
    alone at eight
one morning on the roof I was asleep
and felt your body climb on me. You climbed the ladder
    to the roof, lifted the blanket, ate
my mouth. My tree found rain. You cried. I keep
your sorrow. Happy Sunday long ago. Fire in a morning
    of surprise, and far off Popo's smoke.

The Lilies

The lilies in the field below a sphere
of half moons in the rain, of fowls and moths,
go unclothed, do not spin or toil or hear
the prayer of Solomon in radiant cloths
and yet their nakedness is perfect snow
under whose milky galaxies the seed
lies comatose. The lilies only grow
and burn. Their meditation is to feed
on light. Naked of thought, a multitude
by the day Adam learned to stand, these plants

are human, living in chance villages
like breezy monks sworn to dumb elegance.
When thrown into the oven, no lord says
a word. The lilies fall in solitude.

Ten-Minute Snuff Drama

Argentina. Not the Dirty War. Just a back room
in an apartment in the outskirts of the city
where a blonde Italian whore is being filmed
by a crew of two crab-eyed hoodlums. Art, craft,
            goodness, pity,
none of these qualities crosses the eyes
of the hoodlum filmmakers. Greed
and a hardness to kill any guilt or humanity
      they might feel lies
like a knife slash across their faces. A Romeo
      waltzes in. He strips. Then strips
      the blonde. He keeps
his black belt on from which hang revolver
      and lasso, gaucho style. Romeo is ridiculous.
      Then he moves his stiff prick near
her mouth, feeds it to her. If she had any sense
she would bite it off, spit the pink head
      on the floor and stamp on it
till her soles sucked up every drop of blood.
He almost comes. She's doing a good job
in getting him worked up. They're standing,
      he's pawing her breasts. "Más, más! More,
      more! But the actor pulls out,
      yanks out his gun with the blanks,
and whispers, "Pucha madre! No more obscenities,
little one. I'm here to clean up the city, wipe out
a dirty whore. Get ready to die."
"Don't shoot," she begs, remembering the script.

"It's my duty. And besides, this gun is real."
"Real as this film," she ad libs.
"Say your prayers."
"Cut!" she shouts. "That's not the script."
"Say your prayers, little whore cunt. The good guys
have tickets and are waiting to watch you drop."
The tall Italian whore stops. She's no fool.
"I think you mean it."
"I mean it."
She doesn't beg now. She surprises Romeo.
"If you kill me, you will be executed. Go ahead,"
    she baits him.
"Cunt! Fry in your own grease."
"Go ahead. I've nothing to lose, but the law
    will execute you. I guarantee it."
He raises the gun. She grabs his balls ferociously.
He falls, clutching himself. She fights for the gun.
They roll. And before she can bend
it from his hands, Romeo sticks it in her mouth
and blows her head off. What's left of the female
    figure lies still. Dead ethnic vermin.
Order and civilization have won.
The hoodlums cheer. End of battle. Peace.

THE END

Goya and Rembrandt Stroll on 23rd

Goya takes 23rd Street since he knows
those bodies huddled by the wall to keep
their warmth. He bathes them in brown ink. Their clothes
are soaked. His crucifieds sprawl in a sleep
of stonemen. Goya puts them under wrap,
except their eyes—candles in rain—which look
up from the pavement for a starry map
of hope. They lie by dogshit in the book

of night and vomit. Rembrandt finds a face
of angels in the alley. Neon lights
in the store window of the liquor store
ignite his lady's skin. A holy space.
The masters catch Manhattan's chilly whore
and panhandler in blankets and black tights.

Two Souls Meet on a Windy Night and Worry
about a Marble Face

After the war when we were young and gray in heart,
I went to Paris to get exiled, kiss a soul, and hear
    the wind
blowing the urine fragrance along Bonaparte.
Stiff black coffee and warm bread were my early copains.
    Wind dozed among the lindens.
I let it share my bed. The bed was bare;
a torn red blanket under a gray bulb of maybe
    30 watts, if I can count,
sputtered high on the ceiling, blinking at my underwear
dripping and wrinkled on the sink edge. I read
    the philosophy of Auguste Compte
hard as I could at the Sorbonne until my prof,
Monsieur La Porte, dropped dead. La Porte est fermée
was cruelly scribbled on the door. I met a soul
one windy night. Paris embraced us with her laugh.
She was a Greek. She gave me an ancient statue that hurt
my arms. The cheekbones almost pierced the skin.
    It's so heavy, where can I put it down? I say
to her.
    Don't ever put it down, she says. We Greeks wake
    with a glaring
marble head in our arms. Hold it up or it will roll
    away.

Rendezvous

Father, you are the phantom of the opera
and not for being a jumpy ghost, insane
or criminal, but you disclose an algebra
of living infinite and zero, plain
and complex, on a stage of dreams. I'm old
enough to be your uncle since you died
so far ago, but you insist on hold-
ing on to us. It's good. And though I've tried
to face your exit, love says no. I yield
to you. Your violent plunge was just the end
but we dream back through our companionship,
warmer and wilder. Daytime, you're concealed.
A sad convention. Come dark sleep, you slip
into my shirt. We talk all night, sweet friend.

Dancing in the Tower

I have become a creature of myself,
sitting downtown in the Encore Café,
reading a book or writing one. My wolf
waits for me in the garage while I stray
into an intermission. Some folks greet
me, I greet back. I'm friendly and alone
and used to it. Mornings are grim. I meet
the copulating mirror, put a milkbone
in the wolf's bowl, tell him goodbye. I'm stale
on my mail run, but hole up happy in
my tower. My books are sitting in this park,
I love them, I've become them. They blackmail
me and I pay off. Go home? Why? I've been
there once. Right now I'm dancing in the dark.

Blindman

I move, guess I'm alive, and wake because
the sun is orderly. But I was bad
again, scrawling all night until the laws
of body felled me. I cruised to my pad,
a rag, happy. Still a rag, I've become
a coffee bag to stay awake. When night
shoots me again by janitors, I'm glum
but burn my shoes. Once inside my block of light
mechanically I dream of Paris rain
and dance for no one, dance a bit insane,
looking nowhere. How dreary in this jail
for an old dog of habit in white trance
of elsewheres to be jumping wild in braille!
The difference between death and life is dance.

Loneliness

The loneliness intensifies the fact
and dream. I talk to me. I'm not a bore
and when I dream as Daniel dreamt and act
with faith like Shadrach, even though I snore
the Babylonian furnace cannot singe
my hair. But I am sick of miracle
or waiting for the sun to cool orange
so I can climb and camp on that black hill
of light the way Plotinos would if he
could get a foot onto his mystic star.
It's been a good cold rainy day. I talk
all night to me. Dreaming up a Zohar
to lamp my way to peace, blindly I see
no shore of silence as I walk and walk.

Existing Is Strange

I always thought that time would fill the hole
of being and I'd no longer be a ghost.
I never knew I'd played the normal role
of human with a brain. What scared me most
was when I found I was just a pink sack
of flesh ballooned with Eastern nothingness.
Am I the only one to watch the black,
and worse, the non-interior of this mess?
I always thought that on a rainy day,
maybe a Saturday with no one home
and loneliness a cave, I'd spot a deep
and plunging drop of mind like a snow ray
from hell. One Paris afternoon this dome
of nothing almost shone, but then came sleep.

Laughing is Real, but around the Corner Comes
Black Wind

Anton Chekhov died young and yet he wrote
ten thousand pages and trudged all across
Siberia to the prisoners in remote
notorious labor camps. They froze. Their loss
of hope was total. Lashes and disease
were everyday. He spoke and healed and gave
us word. He knew our secrets and the ease
of wasted lives. I'm secretive and crave
exactly what he was. He's dead. But not
tonight. Tonight I feel my death will stare
at me before I'll chat with secret you
the way that doctor warmed the world. He thought
suffering bad, found no escape. I declare
my love for you. Tough luck. Nothing comes true.

The Secret Friend

I am surprised to find you at the end
of our strange walk. You stick with me, although
I'm dead, or else obscure, and I depend
on you, the unknown friend, for life. Spino-
za built a world with words, dressing his tree
with letters of infinity. He ground
his lenses with a love that couldn't see
the one they fit with vision, and the sound
of the mute cosmos was his sole return
for love. I've been too lonely to survive
on nature or the wild and singing shark,
and shaped my life and manuscript to earn
your gaze. Sun burns up thought, yet in the dark
inside, I pause to meet your eyes alive.

Dog Poems and Ghost Ballads   1997

In Miguel de Cervantes's *Colloquy of the Dogs,* two dogs spend the night in a courtyard gossiping and eventually tell us the magnificent fable, *The Man of Glass.* Dogs have always talked, since they are older than Pharaohs and Chinese emperors. Yet these literary dogs, like Franz Kafka's beetle, have a human tongue under their beast shell. Then there are ordinary dogs, the ones who sniff grass, whose natural speech is a bark, a whine, or a Tibetan monk's low prayer growl. We can translate their utterances into words, but the original is better. In their authentic state, these dogs are teachers and earth angels. In them reside song, suffering, companionship, and little complaint. Earth angels don't bitch.

—Pierre Grange, "Canine Genealogy"

Standing in the Rain

Monday morning I put out the garbage.
April downpour. Buck looks at me quizzically.
"Is it a walk with me or are you lonely?

hauling plastic balloons of leaky trash
and need a friend?" You come. I need a friend.
Since the car hit you it is hard to walk

Olympic fast, so you raise the hurt leg
in hunger pause and ballet slowly to
my side. We don't get far when you stand in

the woods, letting the rain launder your coat
and dissolve the mud caking your nose.
I laugh. Not only Lord Elgin stole marble

out of Greece, since here in blue woods,
I'm chatting with a breathing wolf who took
refuge in Thera before the volcano blew

and buried the Bronze Age island. I've fleeced
the Mediterranean of a classical beast
Sotheby-priced at two Bach toccatas, a ton

of Parian marble, and a truckful of cracked
Puccini hearts. Bucky in the rain
is vitally here. He's standing. He tells me,

"WillBill, let us agree to let time stop.
I like my biscuit bones, but you, not I,
indulge in illusions. I'm wet and real."

"You win, you beast." I breathe and let the world
go hang itself. the rain incautiously
wets us. Papers in my drowned pockets blur

to watercolor. Buck thins in his soaked
shrinking fur coat. He looks at misty me.
"Chill out," he says. "You'll live. It's only rain."

A Biped and Quadruped's Last Walks

The panther is the handsomest of quadrupeds
from Bishop Theobald's *Bestiary*

Peaceful, sunny, humid Indiana noon,
you, my eager quadruped, are out of
          the hospital cage

and out on the road of pleasures. Eden is
eternal senses cut by time. Expulsion will
          come Tuesday morning.

To cut you free of cancer you will become
a Han dynasty bronze wine vessel filled
          with delicious spirits.

The *American Heritage Dictionary* has
your picture on page 1914: an amazing
          Chinese bronze tripod

enduring after 3,100 years as
a functional vessel of beauty. It
          may be hard to pee,

but you will outlast the director of
the FBI and, with your tricorn hat
          of authority, chase

away any lousy punk who come to
check the meters or hymn the virtues of
        life insurance. Now

a trinity reigns: you, me, and whoever
like us lives in solitude. It's peacefully
        beautiful. Let's run.

The trident sun touches our neck. You lick
the clouds and your wet flashing teeth
        trot through the heart.

The Morning Sun Is a Little Drier

The morning sun is a little drier
        and no one is here
        as we almost secretly

enjoy our last walk on six legs.
        I am weeping (I do
        it easily at tearjerker

films) and you're too busy with great
        news from Paradise grass
        and trees. But you stop

and flash me soulwet sympathy
        through brown-smart eyes,
        being gentle with me;

then snap alert in hunter beauty
        and trot in the woods.
        Dry sun gives you pep,

you wade in a ditch pool and sprawl
    and slurp up rain.
        Blue thistles and Queen

Anne's lace watch I'm scrawling on
    a Bank One check,
        dragging along. You

check out a snow pine and sit under
    it. This is the life.
        Tomorrow the saw

A white butterfly. Day crickets hear
    us. You sprawl
        your limbs handsomely,

calm wolf meditating before combat
    in the Roman Coliseum,
        and peer at butterflies,

waiting for the high ghost in white
    coat and white mask
        to step out on the sand

with the knockout needle of sleep,
    the rubber fingers
        and the amputating blade.

Sloppy Good Friday Night

There rose a tree. Robert has come. Buck sang.
    He sings like the deer wind
        in the blue Sinai desert, the gazelle

hopping silently along the far hill slope.
  My dog chants low like bromide
  on the salt mush by the Dead Sea,

and as he swashes Rob's face Bucky rolls high
  like birds, surviving dinosaurs,
  who bellow from the newly risen tree.

Then we take a short walk. His hips are weak
  but walking gives him speed.
  I wait. Buck too. When I go in he stays,

sitting. It's a lovely evening. Maybe in
  an hour he can chew on moon
  breeze. The night out is a cinch. And fun.

Up in the barn Robert has crashed. I'm gone
  to sip juice in my solitude
  place. Buck gave me a look when he lay

on the stairs that tossed a brown boomerang
  over the Pacific into my guts.
  Now he's outside. I brood on his fresh sleep.

Ghost Ballads

Velvel Bornstein in the Warsaw Ghetto

I am a starving child. Outside
          The gate the garbage stands
In cans. My father said to hide,
Not let the Germans get their hands

On me, but I can't stand it, so
                I slip outside the gate
At sundown. I am like a crow
Pecking away at crumbs. It's late

And I try to sneak back, but a
                Nice soldier grabs my arm
And picks me up. I'm miles away
From fear. It feels so far from harm

To have a healthy tall man hold
                Me in his arms. He takes
Me to the center of the road
And talks to me. Carefree, he shakes

Hands with a buddy, grabs me tight
                Again, and tighter. Then
He starts to hug me and I'm light
And happy, yet my oxygen

Begins to fade. I realize
                He's choking me. I bite
His wrist. I kick. His giant size
Subdues me and I lose the fight.

I'm dead. He carts me to a man-
                hole, lays me on the ground,
Opens it up, shoves all he can
Till I am drifting underground

In the black sewer under the square.
                Bronislaw Zielinski sees
Me drown. Years later exactly where
I died, Bron tells my agonies

To an American in War-
            saw, who has come to be
My witness. That Jew and visitor
Is writing this. He could be me.

Billy Bones on the Street

Manhattan streets are gray with gangs
Of kids in knickers just like him,
And after twilight Billy hangs
Around, lonely but never grim.

He skirts the Catholic church of stone,
The movie house of shining brass,
The temple where the Jews atone,
The liquor bar where girls show ass.

He's off to see his Boy Scout master
Down in the 70s on West End.
It's almost eight, he's late, and faster
Skipping, he's running with no friend

To keep him safe. There's no one on
The spooky street, but in his head
He's pumping flags—twilight is gone—
To pass his semaphore. He's read

The book, he's practiced every night,
He's got it nailed, yet then three guys
Surround him, looking for a fight.
His head is elsewhere but he tries

To run. They tackle him. He hits
The pavement on his face. It hurts.
They stick three knives in him. He spits
Out gobs of blood. One tough guy squirts

A water pistol filled with piss
Against his torn-up nose. Where is
His master's face? He starts to miss
His mom and dad. He was a whiz

In school—where is Miss Howard now
When he is croaking in the street?
But one punk has an ice pick, and wow!
(Before Bill spots the bully), neat

With a mean fist he blinds the jerk,
Adding more pain for fun. Now when
The cops find Billy in the murk
of dawn, he's still alive. The men

Pick up the wounded kid and toss
Him in their van. Billy looks sad
Yet pumps his arms. He's got to pass
His semaphore or he'll die bad.

Teddy Monobomber

While tough kids in Chicago played
At supper baseball in the street
Or dreamed desserts of getting laid,
Young Ted made chemicals his sweet.

He mixed delicious nitrates up,
Smoothies of mercury and salt;
He boiled them in an iron cup
And patented his poison malt.

And Teddy was a grand gourmet
Of radium gleaming hot. For math
He counted out the Milky Way
And mixed its stardust in his bath.

As Ted grew brightly as a man
He worked his way through school,
Taking his doc in far Japan
Where no one countenanced a fool.

There Ted was in his glory days.
He found a job and made a mint
Yet in the evenings came the craze
Of loneliness. He chewed a mint

And stayed inside. He hated Japs,
He hated USA. He crawled
Back home, fuming. It looked like taps
For every hope, and Teddy bawled.

Yes, Ted was sad. He never had
A girl to love. It was a shame
For such a genius to be mad
All day and brood at night on blame.

He blamed the university
And government, ditched his career
To live alone in poverty,
In bible wilderness all year.

And soon he was a monk, a saint
Of hatred for the public sin
Of industry and greed. No taint
Of joy was found in his cold inn.

He worked. God how he worked! and used
His tiny instruments (he made
Them all himself). Ted never boozed
Or spent a fast night getting laid.

He knew the world would listen to
His holy words—even his mom.
He had to wake them from their zoo
And so he labored on his bomb.

And when he built the biggest blast
A man could fit into a box,
He mailed it to himself, the last
Good man on earth. He was the fox

Amid the sheep. He cared, he dared,
The planet needed him to save
Its stupid soul, and Ted despaired
That even he might not be brave.

The lightless night was deathly cold
In high Montana where he schemed
His letter to the world. He told
His soul his mission was supreme,

And, as a martyr, once he blew
Himself to newsy smithereens,
The world would read his treatise through
And leap redeemed like jumping beans.

When morning came, he went to get
The mail. The box was there! He tried
Shouting fierce words, not to forget
His quest. Ted wept, opened and died.

Horror spread everywhere. A sage
And prophet, a lonely ideologues,
Had scrawled his visionary page.
To save the world he died a dog!

But every scrap of paper round
That lethal prank proved the offender
A monobomber underground,
Some cold, demonic high-tech sender.

That evening of the mighty bomb,
The media had no clue who'd kill
Good Teddy in his shack. His mom
And FBI swore they would drill

To China—and farther still—just
To nab his killer, spill him dead.
Yet Ted's white sermon blew to dust
In the letter bomb Ted mailed to Ted.

Poor Ted. That angry Cain was lost
In the explosion. What a sad
Twist for Ted who died double-crossed
By his technology gone mad!

Jessica, a Child Pilot, 1996

I am only seven but I fly
        For joy. Sure, I'm a whizz
At chess and blow a sax, yet I'd die
        Before I'd let the fizz

Of fame, the dream of cloud and dome,
        Go flat like a dead coke
Abandoned in its Styrofoam.
        Am I too small? Bad joke.

Must I wait till I'm big and fat
        Like you? Not me. I like

It now. I'm lucky like a cat
                    Climbing the sky. I hike

Above the mist and there I sit
                    On moving air alone,
And floating everywhere, a bit
                    Of night and stardust bloom

Far in the heavens. I've got guts
                    And drift right to the ledge
Of the blind universe that cuts
                    The world in two, the edge

Of light and vacant black. Thrilled, there
                    I fly through deepest dream.
Oops! Now I must prepare to snare
                    The record, get on the beam,

Be sharp and speed us safely high.
                    My dad is here. It's cold
And pouring and the thundering sky
                    Is thick with hail, but gold

Sunshine is waiting for us once
                    Our altitude is right.
"Climb in and grab the joystick," grunts
                    The pro. My dad is bright

And proud in the back seat. I love
                    Him and he thinks me hot
Stuff, neat, a record kid. I shove
                    My foot on the break, knot

My brain to the controls, and let
                    The prop spin faster, test-
ing, testing. "Let 'er go! Now get
                    Us off the ground!" I'm best

When it is worst. This morning's bad.
  No plane is in the sky.
We have a mission and I'm mad
  With passion. Don't ask why

I comb the clouds with steady heart.
  The rain won't kill my chance
In life to be a daring part
  Of fame, to race and dance

Over our planet in the air,
  In our own asteroid,
A bird of wonder. Yet where are
  We now, tossing in void?

I'm scared. We're pitching back
  And forth and plunging down.
I think I'm pretty young. My back
  Is breaking and I'm drown-

ing in my blood. It isn't fun.
  Dad, help! I want to grow
Up tall. No! Don't let the hot sun
  Die. Save me! Dad! No! No!

Sweet Joan of Hearts

After my nurse, the girl along the Drive
  I loved and dreamt of most
Sat on a statue on Street 105.
  Limeys burned her to toast.

Joan was a knight in armor like a man
  And sat erectly on
Her horse. Her lovely eyes studied the plan
  Of heaven where she'd gone

To hear the voice of God and Catherine
Begging, "Save *douce* France
From Burgundy and England." With a grin
She pointed her bronze lance

Into the mist. I loved her true and deep
And would have gone to war
To fight near her by day—and cast my sleep
On paradise's star.

I lingered many afternoons to talk
With her. Grew up and went
To Paris where I trailed her like a hawk,
Hoping by accident

I'd spot her on her horse. In a hotel
On Rue Jacob I took
A room. The concierge shook and gave me hell:
"You are a murderous crook,

You Englishman." "No, I'm American,"
I told the angry crone.
"But you speak English, from that very clan
Of thieves who killed our Joan."

"I'm innocent," I stammered. And went out
For air. I walked the park
Of Luxembourg, sat down, began to pout:
"Where is my Joan of Arc?"

I whimpered, pondering her martyrdom
And she was just nineteen
When she affirmed she was no common scum,
Yet they poured gasoline

On her to flame her at the stake. The saint
    Flew quickly to her end.
Just then a hustler sauntered by to paint
    A picture of his friend,

Who looked like Joan. I knew he was a shit
    And sent him on his way,
While I wept for my love. I used to sit
    Behind her, and one day

On her bronze saddle I slipped my hand in
    Under her armor. Oh,
How hot she was that afternoon! My chin
    On her neck, long ago,

Yet now in these Jardins, I guess she must
    Be nineteen just like me;
It's night, and she perceives my holy lust
    And grave virginity.

Poor Joan, poor me! Yet there is justice when
    I hear her call: "Guillaume!"
And crazy I respond, shouting "Amen!"
    To the far Pope in Rome.

Sweet Joan of Hearts, I loved you as a child
    When you wore sheets of bronze
Up on the Drive. And now I am a wild
    Man. No. We're two wild swans,

And wearing just your naked flesh of France,
    You stare at heaven while
I wet your orchid with my singing lance
    And we float down the Nile.

Father in the Spring

Father, you come to me in spring,
In fragments where I hear you sing,

Caruso lying proudly in the tub,
Soaping, scrubbing, crooning *rub-*

a-dub, and I burst in. You laugh.
You always laugh with me. We're half

A cake together. But you leave
For good when I am ten. I grieve

Because I'll never know you in
The house again. I try to win

You back. You come and stay a year
And it's more precious since I fear

You'll soon go off. You do. But then
We write and call and meet again,

And one whole summer I'm with you.
We're at the Greystone. You are blue.

At first. You've lost your business and
Are down to selling Swiss watchbands,

But by summer's end you're on
You're on your feet, trading diamonds.

Years pass, and in New York I come
On weekends when you're back with some

Free hours. I bring you three Van Goghs,
We have a beer. The spring time throws

Me in a crazy mood. The best
For us. But you are broke. The West

Put silver in your hands and took
It back. You rushed it. Now I look

At you with sorrow. We will meet
Next week. Even if we hit the street

Together, we will overcome.
I'm back in Maine. "Come now. Please come,"

You ask. "I can't until the term
Is over." I talk rather firm,

Surprising me. "Goodbye." I hear
The phone go dead. You disappear

About ten days. I'm on the course
With friends from Mexico. I'm hoarse

From shouting. Back in the blue dorm
Where Hawthorne lived, a sudden storm

Explodes outside. It's nothing. Soon
Be gone. But I am on the phone

With Colorado, a poor line.
"Your father jumped and broke his spine.

He's dead. He jumped off of the roof
Down seven floors." The spring gave proof

Again of its great force. In May,
In lovely May, we split. Your day

Saw you float terrible with grief
I'll never know. There's no relief

For me, which is a good. It keeps
You close. Constantly your dive leaps

Into my sleep, but in my bed
Is where you live. I dream. Your head

Appears. We're swimming in the Sea
Of Galilee. It's nice to be

Out in the middle. You frogkick
Beside me as we chat. "We'll lick

This silly problem of your death,"
I say. You smile. In the same breath,

I hear Caruso. What a dog,
Horsing around with light! I jog

To shore. Soon it's Tibet, Shanghai,
Exotic, safe. I ask you why

You haven't changed. "The soul does not
Lose light." I hope you're right. But what.

You are in me (and I am blank)
Is you. You're with me now. I thank

The foolishness of life that let's
Us joke. I like to laugh. My bets

Are you'll outlast me. What can I do?
I've had a sad time without you.

I have an awful voice. I can't sing.
Caruso, sing for me next spring.

Moonbook and Sunbook   1997

New Moon

The new moon rose, the old moon in her arms.
I am an old moon jogging in the night,
blissfully panting out to strawberry farms.
Jogging isn't a sin. Age is the blight
of nature, yet I'll smooch and dream, a dog
in paradise, pissing on clouds until
I croak. I push the body as I jog,
hoping it won't break up. I'd rather spill,
downed by a busted heart than a soft chair.
No choice. I'm terrified by mind, not death,
as I spot dark inside me. Stars came soon
after a week of rain and gray nightmare
of months. Now racing night thrills me with breath.
Once gone I'll spin my laps on the black moon.

On the Moon

The sun lay on the chalky marble when
I stepped on her. It was too late to blast
up like an astronaut. The moon was ten-
der with my secrecy. She saw me cast
away all sense and safety for a walk
on her. I hiked inside her lakes. The tears
of seas were gone. Lonely, I tried to talk
with her. My wolf dog barked. The moon's thin ears
received us as if Bach were singing for
his Lord. Her hilly breasts were everywhere
and generous. The black in me was milk
and peace, deep as a burning moth. Her floor,
the belly of the sky, dressed me with care.
I slept with her and soaked her loving silk.

The Moon Can Never Know

The moon can never knows she is the moon,
nor sun know he is sun. The minaret
is deaf, the muezzin yells, the faithful swoon
        inside the Tangier mosque, and yet
I talk to her—a blue scimitar in
the pot mist smelling over the city.
I was young in those Casbah days. My sin
        was deep, like now, but don't pity
any Willis. He's stressed, but doesn't know
        remorse. Can the moon feel guilt? No,
        she's faithful. Never lets me down.
She's far, inert, reminds me of dead stone
        and yet I love her. She is beautiful,
        old, empty, new, and makes me full.

A Kid Making It with the Hudson Moon
Who Was a Savvy Dame

When I ran home into the polar wind
booming along the street, the moon was calm
and almost still, a yellow peach who sinned
naked and lusciously over the lamb
of gully snow. She stood perfect above
the Hudson River, her vagina warm
as the fat taxis where the dopes in love
made out, speeding along the Drive. No harm,
I thought, and Eliot could prove those odd -
balls grabbed each other's tits and prick. No one
could look inside, except the sphere who flew
nearby. I heaved onto my bed, my rod
was steel, my eyes a mess of fire and fun.
The lady in the sky, I kissed her blue.

Moonbird

The Persians say she is the nightingale
of memory. Although she's never heard,
her song persists through windows of a jail
or childhood eyes. Unlike the poet's bird
she's visible most every night, and when
a cloud or sunshade blocks her out, we see
her memory in Leopardi, in his pen,
he too a burning virgin. Ecstasy
of standing elsewhere was their common plight
and beautiful escape from solitude.
Shining without oxygen, a stone mirror
her brain, the moonbird knows each single night
of history. Alexander in the nude
draws maps under her breasts and dreams of terror.

Moon Dropping into Our Secret Dutch Attic, 1943

Moon, you catch oceans, glitter them with sun
you flash out from your face, but I am down
here and see just these attic beams. No one
to slip me from this room. You coat each town
with brilliance, but you keep your body clean,
untouched by smoking death camps far below
your gaze. When you are thin, a safety pin
of sexual light, I grab your beams and sew
them in my pockets. I Anne found a hole
through the closed shutters in my attic. When
night locked me in, I saw your drop of bread
and turned it into ink, and your dead soul
was mine. Your brilliance through my oxygen
gives me light hope before I join the dead.

Moonshower in Her Tub of Earth

I like to shower with the moon and do
it early while she's bright and full. I glide
into her tub. She's glistening; and true
to form she takes me to her hidden side.
We close our eyes. The water fills her cracks
and hills and in the shadow we embrace.
Rolling together, moon and earth, our backs
the surface of a deep celestial space
of utter loneliness, we press and cling
tighter not to fall out or disappear.
We dance. The moon is candidly in love
with me. I soap her crevices and sing,
and she, squeezing me to her atmosphere,
drops me, beams me, crushes me from above.

Only a Paper Moon in Argentina During the Dirty War

Mario and I talked ourselves blue guns talked
in Buenos Aires Mario Kabbalah
Dirty War after his lecture we walked
to the Saint James Café the algebra
of mystics Juan de la Cruz Mario knew
the numbers Jesus called by Galilee
to turn the waters into doves a Jew
performed his miracles it was only
a paper moon outside but witness of
the plateless Ford that rounded up some men
and threw a woman in its trunk I heard
the woman scream we couldn't help no love
of miracle or numbers helped again
the paper moon witnessed the disappeared.

Invisible Moon

Antonio Machado said that love
lies in its absence. I see you almost
each night, which makes you the bright princess of
our virgin dates, since sight lies on the coast
of the impossible, and see, not touch,
is how we meet. But usually I day-
dream you—by night and sometimes day—with such
absurdly real intensity, I lay
my body on your dust. I'm not a prop-
er man. While you are waning, while your bell-
y slips to semi-darkness, half-seen space
unknown, I am a cat sneaking on top
of you, a handless pianist on your face,
and hump the evening in your white hotel.

Moonsleep

Year after year I've wanted her and come
to empty fields with cloudless firmaments,
and with my naked eye I soon become
a lunatic abandoning the sense
of time. The moon is infinitely near,
a step away. I touch her toes, her soft
and empty mountains. In her Buddha ear
her gold ravines are literate. I cough
up courage and plunge in. She wel-
comes me. Her dazzling grace lightens my head.
As I worm into her complacent face,
she feels like heaven, she is cold as hell.
Vanishing into her orgasmic space,
I sleep on her, in light. Time of the dead.

Moon Lunacy Escape

I love the moon and so was slapped in jail,
escaped, hunted, and, when the bloodhounds
picked up the scent, got caught, held without bail
until a trial for lunacy had found
me guilty of moon love and negligence
of normalcy. I loved the new moon once
in Egypt. I was meeting common-sense
Ibrahim, my grave-robber friend who hunts
antiquity, a patriarch and seer
of marketable beauty, who sells the eye
of the small sphinx. We met, shared a beer.
I bought the moon. Cheap. His two wives were pissed.
Enraged he shot his pistol at the sky,
but I escaped, the moon safe in my fist.

The Moon Is Sick

The moon is sick. I fear she'll die
from lack of love, from poverty
and homelessness, lost in the sky,
our daughter dropping down the sea
of negligence. And who will glow
on walkers in the night? The moon
will glow and nobody will know
although her name and white balloon
will look the same. But she'll be gone.
Scholars will say, "She went. She was
an obscure custom of a race
of fools." The moon is sick, and on
the crackled face, a pox, a buzz
of priests are nailing her in place.

Scrawling in Cafés and Dreaming Up
a Moon Feast in Her Delicious Kitchen

A lousy cook, I burn water or forget the eggs
till they explode and hit the ceiling like
buckshot. So I haunt cafés. My legs
are European and take me on my bike
to every table in the city. There,
tired of caffeine but glad to read or write
in solitude, I spend my years. I fear
a guilty past, worry about the sight
of faces I must face; my heavy being
can't sleep. Yet when I'm sitting by a fish
and scrawling, then I'm moonglad. Overhead
the moon has her delicious kitchen. Seeing
her—even in my mind—I dream a dish,
her face of yogurt, honey, cheese and bread.

Moonblasted

I'm writing sonnets to the moon, yet all
is Humpty Dumpty tumbling down. Okay.
I'm fine, although the college library called
to say it's quits. You can't take books today
or ever. Health insurance cut. Out of
control. That's life. I can't get it together,
papers a mountain, sleep a worry. Love
is everywhere, so why complain? My mother
told me to scrub the sink after I washed
the dishes. Why didn't that metaphor
sink in? I'm writing sonnets to the moon,
who helps me get up from the dismal floor
of going broke. I'm crazy as a loon,
a piece of joy, moonblasted and light-squashed.

Prairie Rose Moon

The prairie rose moon blowing on the glass
of heaven hangs a moment on a bud
of fire. A windy angel. I am pass-
ing through. Her dignity, like Billy Budd
swinging forever from the mast, compels
her permanence of rolling flame. I stare.
Her colors signify what Shakespeare tells
photographers: 'Click, but I will not bare
my real identity. Stick to my light
and leave my blood and face alone.' I guess
I'm like the rest. I want to know. Perhaps
because I don't know me inside (a mess
of words ticking to dead-end night), by night
I see her rose with hope and then collapse.

Spinoza Gapes at the Moon through Glass
He Ground in the Amsterdam Ghetto

Isn't it good to believe space? I wish
that space were life. Spinoza made his moon alive
because he had to find God everywhere. A fish
or planet or a lens he ground to dive
into the heart where he could study soul
whose light is numbered rain. Caligula
ordered his slaves to catch the moon and roll
it to his throne. I own that cupola
laughing in heaven, and I'm not a nut
or wiseman. I just look and she is mine.
My ghetto moon is laced with chocolate cream
with whom I talk and sleep. She feeds me dream.
Spinoza didn't kid himself. He cut
his soul in Latin glass so soul could shine.

Goya's Moon

Yard with Madmen 1793-1794
oil on tinplate

Franciso Goya's little yard with mad
men lives in gloom under a yellow sky.
The caretaker horsewhips the naked bad
embracing lunatics. Moon in their eye.
Goya by now is deaf. The men are globs
of paint and lack the balance to conceal
an insane moon in all of us. Their throbs
and inner gales derange their eyes and steal
their right to live outside the yard and wall.
Goya is free. He breaks all rules and saves
me from illusions that I might be sane.
Mad Goya paints the truth of fear, the ball
of hope that soars into the clouds and raves,
and falls on fire into his moonlit brain.

Moonray in a Mexican Graveyard, 1945

She is a blast. I like to go on dates
with her. I'm a young squirt. She has no age.
In Miacatlán we are three village mates
lying by blue ceramic graves. But sage
and bright, she doesn't kick up a storm
at our ménage à trois. We hug. She tattoos
romantic light across our chests. Our form,
the two-backed beast of love, is new
to us. Round, trembling, our sweet milk and sweat
grow brilliant as we shake the world away
and come to secret knowing. In Mexico
a graveyard is a private place. We let
night's mercy govern us, in moon shadow
by Nahua tombs, collapsing in one ray.

Patient Moon

The moon is not impatient like the son
of man who cleaned the lepers, and the eye
around the planet washes her green sun
of midnight on a few whose meadows cry
for sperm, maddens the people of the boats
with milk flaming on rock. Yet even when
she floods a dying child, she never floats
out of her crater with the oxygen
of faith, nor lords us with a vision ray
of crystal heaven. Full and filled with sand,
her face is the death object in the night,
is now and nebulous. While mystery and
apocalypse are sleep, her yes of light
glares out of dream to love, our waking clay.

Moon Nurse

Help me. I fear my temples will explode
and beating blood leak out. Everyone begs
your help and you miss none. Climbing your road
of entry, lady bathed in starch, with legs
of stockinged white, you signal to remain
in bed, drink liquids, and obey the rules.
You let me down. I'm not too good at sane
comportment and tonight my body drools
with sweat and colds. But I apologize.
I am ashamed. You are a savior
by rising every night to carry sun
to us. I am about to burst. My eyes
seek other hands to hurl me from a gun
through space to you, but you sneak off and snore.

294

Du Fu Recalling Li Bai and His Moon Swan

December night almost freezes us, but
a bowl of wine, the dishes on the floor
in Ming-bright China, keeps our smelly cot-
tage hot with fun. These days when we are poor,
neither of us holds a post. We both failed
the imperial texts. Imagine asking us
how to compose a poem! Your daughter sailed
to Peach Blossom Spring. The black octopus
of hunger strangled her. My head is white
in mourning for my youth. Good Li, you drink
a lot and write a lot. The moon looks on.
We walk outside. I'm turning blue. You fight
the horror of our villages of ink
on fire, while overhead you spot your swan.

Mooncalm

At twilight a horizon nun
glides about in camomile robes
of clouds over the morose sun.
The new moon in the east disrobes,
a naked Burmese woman thin
before the planet's icy bloom
of stars. She's wonder in her skin
of light, and in her virgin womb
she hold the full moon she will be.
Her adolescent face is al-
ways an astonishment. To know
is innocence, an ecstasy
of going elsewhere. She is tall
with hope. A slow exquisite glow.

Halfmoon

These woods are green, alive, but have no mind
like the black sun dancing on broken toes.
this halfmoon's not alive, though she is kind
for a dead woman. She's my wife. She knows
nothing of me, yet slips me light. I take
her love, and every night I search her face,
her stony aphrodisiac hips, and stake
my emptiness on her. She rolls in place
since she checked out from Earth. I'm here few years
but we're both aching terribly alone.
That mirror face, I talk to her cold glass.
I love her as I've never loved and fears
for her existence fade. Yet she's a bone
whispering, "Come and join my luminous mass."

Gospel of Black Hats

The spring is late this year. Its winds are raw,
aching a bit. The moon is full. I pad
down through the gully to Salt Creek. The law
of seasons will prevail, ending the sad-
ness of dead grass, and soon my winter in
the barn will end. I fade lonely in space
back to my land next door to a Ukraine
of vast jade fields, strange like the other race
inside the ghetto villages. Black hats
and books in velvet. Of my people? Gone
a century, that blood was me. I pass
and as the grass can't know it is the grass,
I see no wings from mystic chariots,
yet in my blood the moon burns on and on.

Sunbook

for Robert Barnstone
Boston b. 1893
Colorado Springs d. 1946

Pamplona in the Sun

In an outdoor café off Harvard Square,
I'm sitting in the sun, reading the work
of a black waiter who's asking me where
to sell it. Good luck. I too have had to lurk
outside the store, waiting. My soles are thin,
my hair not bad, yet life is time. The sun
would let me come, but it is boiling in
his photosphere. Back on the square a nun
toots her harmonica, a thin guy sits
against the wall, relaxed. HOMELESS WITH AIDS
his sign reports. He's beautiful. His wits
are sharp, I'm sure. It's time for God, it's time
for God to show. Please show. We all are made
of flesh, yet Lord or sun can't spare a dime.

Father Sun Gazing Down from His Kiosk

The father sun is friendly with each son,
the Chinese deserts, and camps out on them,
filling the Gobi with oblivion
and yurts, Gnostics, the white freshwater gem
of pearls that fill the push carts in the mar-
kets. On the planet's lowest plain I ran
all morning through the oxygen-rich air,
took breathers in cold streams. There in Xinjang,
old Turkestan, the sun and I were pals.
Under his gaze I wrestled with a Turk,
shared soup, walked to an abandoned white mosque,
eyeball of mystery by the night canals
of tyranny as in Tibet. The clerk
of heaven, punctual star, laughed in his kiosk.

Napping in Boston in the Hot Sun

In Boston gentle sun glows on the phlox
and zinnias in this public park. The Jap-
anese are snapping pictures of me, the fox
among the Latin sheep. I like to nap
along the rows of flowers sucking the sky.
I'm so excited I must play the blind
man, close my eyes, and be the summer fly
a hand will sweep away. The sun is kind
to madmen and the poor: a democrat,
Walt Whitman among pigeons or San-
cho Panza joking on Castilian plains.
My sun is blind to ethnic habitat,
and while I breathe he greets me as a swan
of hope. But when I'm dead, he'll cheer my pains.

Comrade Sun

Comrade sun, why aren't you well behaved
like a calm moon (who's stormy once in a
green moon)? You roar, you burn, you hurt. I'm saved
from malice by averting your deathray
of flame into my eye. The waters gleam
next to Longfellow Bridge, and almost nude
joggers and cyclists soak you up. I *seem*
to be a while. You are. My solitude
longs for your public party face. Don't talk.
Hugging me with your boiling arms feels good
enough. Dante awoke in Hell and you
came thin on morning hills. In my black wood
of death, you'll laugh at my dim state. This walk
in Boston (where my Dad saw light) will do.

Spooking the Firmament

The universe is such a waste   *   I read
its beauty in dominions of far sparks
which are more dream than fire   *   On our blue bead
of earth I waste my breath   *   jogging on parks
until one year I'll join the waste of flesh
under the earth   *   while those brown dwarfs and moons
and bigger stars are dumb without one fresh
cucumber or a woman's tongue   *   Some tunes
of Mozart's piano ping across the brow
of Mercury   *   that's all a spaceship can
cook up to gentrify infinities
of sand   *   But now I'm falling off this cow
of grass   *   out to a void   *   a fisherman
wondering what soul I'll drag up from dead seas   *

Van Gogh's Sun

At George School I bought three cheap Van Gogh prints
and sent them to my father who framed them
in Colorado. They found his footprints
next to the iron stairs. The sunflower stem
held Vincent's burning eyes seizing a vision
of Provence, pigments, friendship, modest sale
and fame. When Dad ceased to be the magician
from Mexico, he walked to the black rail,
leaped from the roof and floated like black sun
down to the bloody street. On his office walls
I found Van Goghs. I know he'd hung them there
for me. I'm getting off the sub. Boston.
Climbing the museum stairs where Van Gogh calls
me to reclaim his sun and Father's air.

Father Sun of Romantic Days

My father sun, my father who's not here
(and most of childhood wasn't there), each place
we lived together, walked to was a near
collision of red happiness. Your face
persists in Mexico, on gray Broadway,
on riding deserts of the patient West
in a white Buick. What romantics! Play
and work. War year. Dames and sun. In your vest
you kept a bag of diamonds. From them came
our bread and costs of love. Pour them on blue
velvet and change them magically to green-
backs. Texas night was endless. We became
a long white moon, smashed a deer's ass, and you
and I drove till sun rose sweet and obscene.

Sunbomb and the Eternity of Killing

"We have known sin," Rob Oppenheimer said
after he knew his sunbomb worked. It brought
a bit of photosphere to earth. The dead
light up like sunlight. Hiróshima is hot,
a tiny star pinned on the earth. It weeps,
its star goes out, but radium holds it live
till all the dead have died. The big sun keeps
exploding and the killing fields survive
and glitter. Later, Oppenheimer's hit
and dies as if he too were burned by hell.
There are no moral executions. When
the electric chair works like a hypocrite
to sun a criminal, the graveyards yell
with every shot of flame, "Never again!"

Sunflower

Yellow moon mirror of the sky's fire rock,
you turn your head to your own colored sun
and measure dawn and dayfall like the clock
of heaven till the dead clock's work is done.
At night you cannot dream, although you grow,
alive unlike your sun-twin in the sky.
A plant and gaseous rock, a bride and beau,
a stunning pair, beauty and wonder, the eye
of day and leaf of time, you speak the light
of silence. Both of you are mute. I'm glad
to be your talking friend. That's all I do,
talk and record. But you don't long to right
or wrong the world. You add. One night you clad
China in sunflowers hidden in black dew.

Into May Sun, 1946

You were a self-made man, but you made me
and still make me, though you went long ago.
You had some cash left—for say two cups of tea
and a quick passage down to Mexico,
a futile one. I came down from Maine. We walked
the pavements of New York and didn't sleep
that night, our last one. All night long we talked
and it was grand and bad. The dawn came deep
with worry. You, broken, battered my heart.
I went back north, we talked once more. The call
was bad. I couldn't come. You flew off to
the south. The sun refused to rise. His art
of pleasure wouldn't show. You jumped and all
we were was sun. You're with me even now.

Buddha and the Sun

The Buddha sitting on the sun was not
proselytizing, but taking a nap.
Earlier, seeking enlightenment, the thought
of his dear wife and child, the palace trap
of comfort, almost broke his will to dump
them all, but gods turned earth around so he
saw straight ahead. Siddhartha, now grown plump
with canny vision under the Bodhi Tree,
laid his new holiness on sumptuous sun.
The earth grew dark in spots, a fine eclipse
shaded the forest gardens. Sun felt good,
better than meat or women. When he was done
with sunning, he said thanks, hoisted his ships
and drifted filled with light and became wood.

Yeshua in the Sun

Yeshua the rabbi is nailed on the cross
by occupying Romans. Last sun. But
he doesn't know he isn't human. Loss
of life is agony and big spikes cut
his feet and hands in unbearable pain,
but he is just a Jew who Romans said
was "trouble." Pilate takes the role of Cain
murdering the Semite so he'll be dead
without his blessing or his sheep. At noon
they nail the rebel. Now he cannot leak
in public: "Yeshua's the Messiah," friends
whisper. He doesn't know it, or why Greek
will be his cover name and tongue. He ends
on fire. The night sun fails. Black is the moon.

Sun, Shine on Me

Sun, shine on me. I need you as a horse
needs grass, as mares need mountains and sperm rain
since it is muggy. I'm washed out. My force
has gone to sleep. Yet there it dreams. I'm sane
and have the wildest pictures in my night.
That's normal, isn't it? I live with no regret.
I'm grateful for the moon. I held her light,
she pampered me, we found a spot and wet
the meadow with our love. I lost my watch
in France, the mountain grass absorbed our time
and you came warm to dawnwake us. I need
you, sun. I'm fit and ready. If my crotch
and heart and brain are beggars and I live in slime
and memory, burn my craze. Shine on my greed.

The Dream Below the Sun

> The dream below the sun that stuns and blinds,
> torrid dream at the hour of reddening sky.
> —Antonio Machado (1875-1939)

Why wake to awareness of illusion? Dream,
the normal state, lets time under the sun
perform its act of slipping speech, daydream
and daybeams into our mind like someone
controlling things. The truth of emptiness
is much too painful. Once, I saw the void
and almost slipped away. Enough! The mess
of absence is a boring long tabloid,
screaming: *You are nowhere, no one!* My friend
Antonio Machado knew the blur.
I see his landscapes dream. Interior sky
fills him. In him mountains of Soria send
their snowy backs robed in the sun's white fur.
A sunning bull is better than night's lie.

Miguel and His Midnight Sun

In Spain Miguel de Unamuno at
his desk turns out another desperate tale.
It's midnight and the desk is old and splat-
tered with ink like his hero Manuel
the Good who is a priest and can't believe
in oak trees or a sky of God. The Basque
cranky writer is cold. His grim black sleeve
contains a smaller book. Through it he'd bask
in midnight sun. Yet night gives little hope
of cutting loose from tragic sense. He and
his hero—godless Spaniard fencing death—
need everlasting sun. And while they grope,
Miguel again pens deeper in the sand
below his desk, digging for sun and breath.

Living Alone

To live alone at my age is to be
a quietist, Miguel de Molinos.
I eat my books for breakfast and drink tea
called Morning Thunder. Quiet and the φως –
Greek light – I dream them both, and in a chair
right out of bed I talk out loud, hoping
to see through bone and loaf in frozen air.
All this weirdness is proper Spanish being.
I love what I am not, the mystic Juan
of nothingness who carried sun at night
to walk to unseen love. He was alone,
a woman with her God. I haven't gone
to sleep again, and look, there is no light
inside. I live alone with the unknown.

Sun and Glass

Will you stick with me, sun? I'm made of glass
and you shine through. You shine and I'm alive.
At night I sleep because I know you'll pass
through me again. I need light to survive
above the ground. I'm not a man of gloom,
a downer. Ask my friends. But I'm not well
these days, and locked inside a steamy room,
wanting the sun and not to crack, I smell
the fall. It's long and lovely in this state.
Maybe I am a gloom grub, yet one chance
to eat a watermelon in Kashgar
and I am gone, the gypsy. My odd fate
is nature designated me to dance
the role of me. I'm glass and focus far.

Sun Converting Darkness into Every Mystic's
Dazzling Night

In my dark room I see the sun. It's right
and natural. Sun is in the mind. That's where
it is, even outside. I watch the light
this morning cooling Indiana air
here in the woods, on yellow poplar, oak
(my barn is made of it) and slender beech.
Though ignorant of nature, who will choke
my air to death, I relish her green speech,
her sometime calm. In my dark room the sun
permits me hope. I see and hope. My books
are sun because they convert darkness in-
to every mystic's dazzling night and stun
my fear of dying. The sun like mountain brooks
dazzles and I laugh lost in her cool inn.

Drip of Silence

On the first lazy day of spring I went
outside and sat an hour, eating the sun
for breakfast. Then pulled out the *Times*. I meant
to skim, but saw my obit. It was fun
to have the chance to read about the death
of me, WB. It wasn't cruel:
A young professor killed. I checked my breath.
At least it wasn't suicide. The fool
drowned in a tub. Black sun and silence—just
the overflow—and yet the silence killed
him twice. He'd lost all hope of readership.
Saint Paul phoned me. It helped. He said he'd bust
me in the jaw for my mistakes. I filled
my glass with words. The tub spoke drip drip drip.

The Prodigal Son (Luke 15:11-32)

We were two sons. Father gave me my share
of wealth and soon I gathered a few clothes
and books and took a ship into the glare
of Paris where I spent my loot on booze
and women, and one night of revelry
I got so stoned a thief came to my room,
bagged everything I owned in sheets. With glee
he tapped downstairs and fled. I felt no gloom
and never wrote my folks until I starved
in Spain. By then my father died, and I
came back to search for him. He saw me far
away from where he lay and called, "I carved
a cloud in here for you." "Make me your slave,"
I moaned. "I've sinned. Take me from sun." But he
said, "You my child were dead and now you are
alive," and kissed my tears that washed his grave.

306

Pine Tree Talks to Me Under Green Maine

Dora Barnstone, d. 1955

Why did those pancreatic cells gone bad
parade as half your life? It seized the floor
your early death, as you became a nomad
in the last weeks. You laughed as you left shore
on the Greek liner floating you to Greece.
Then dehydration on the ship, X-rays
in Athens that revealed the hopelessness,
Paris where I met your tears, a few days
in New York. And you sank from sun. Our blind
authorities of soul copped out - the Lord
and Lady up in heaven sipped their tea.
I came from you. You lived alone and signed
out dignified and patient on the board
that coffined you to Maine to be a tree.

Give Me Another Mile with You

I'm sorry for you, Father. Now I know
the belt of fire you wore. I feel it too.
Your demons had you reeling. I can go
another mile. You couldn't make it through
another day and flew into the sun
and darkness. And from pain and light you're free.
I hurt and worry but I'm not yet done
with words and love. You'd be 103
today if you were sitting with me here
alone as you were when you took the stair
up to the roof, the narrow path to death.
Too young. Now I'm your older brother. Stare
at me out of your horror pit nowhere.
I love you. Help me taste each lucky breath.

307

Sun Father, Be More Than a Train Watcher
Who Sat While the Cattle Cars Rolled By

These nights I wonder. Older, I have read
Dickinson amazing the page, her soul
annihilated by Calvinist God
who didn't elect her. You glowed her whole
in white through bedroom curtains. You have seen
her ecstasies and death. You know us all.
You knew my father too. I saw him lean
on you one afternoon next to a wall
in Taxco. His bald pate a gold peso
mirroring glorious escape. You watched him die.
He flew through you. And every morning I
have left, you boom, 'I am your father and
the holy light.' Reading your stunning O,
I chill before indifferent flaming sand.

Innocently Alive

Each child tumbling out on the grass of life,
like the guanaco born in Patagonia,
sees sun, is innocent, and then the knife
cuts free the mother's cord until pneumonia
returns that child to dark. My father saw
the sun on Milk Street, though his mother paid
his birth with death. Some of us fell to law
of ovens like the spinning lily made
to live a day and then be cast to fire,
and some feel guilt for having kept our sun
alive. I'm innocent, and yet I hurt
since one I loved tumbled from the high wire
between two roofs and bloodied his fresh shirt.
He's with me now, trying to greet his son.

Demons

Father, you always said to stand up tall.
It made me happy. We were walking on
a street in Colorado, a sweet fall
before your leap. In August the huge bomb
cremated Hiroshima and the war
was gone. An afternoon in Mexico
in our Quaker peace camp, the radio
reported the exploded sun, the Whore
of Babylon. That fall the demons slept.
We had, as always, just a few good days
and then I wandered East. If you had lived,
what would I be? More confident? Your grace
was bright. Less poet? After your leap I wept
and learned the night. Your tall sun has survived.

Love Tent

Every few years I dig around and find
a letter from my father with the seal
of some hotel he stopped at, going blind-
ly town to town to make himself a deal
and work his way again back up on top.
It's far ago. I'm just like him. I try
to make time work for me, but time the cop
of death will cuff me as he nabbed him. I'll sigh
and go. The sun on that black Monday will
forget to rise, I'll be holed up in bed
yet scrawl a letter back to him. Dad went
except in me. He takes my hand. I fill
his palm of dust with sun. And we're not dead
because we love and chat in his blue tent.

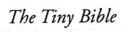

The Tiny Bible

Plato is queer and a scribe

Plato is queer and a scribe to the South Wind heavy
        with rain that soaks painted marble Athens

in January, where he teaches under a plane tree.
        He asks his slaves to spread wild carnations

after his friend Dion, Tyrant of Syracuse, dies.
        "Others honor you with statues and orations

but I loved you," Plato said. Above shadows and flux
        are his fixed forms of Beauty, Sun and Good,

but chained to darkness no sun comes. Think of the boy
        who carried spears for a soldier in battle mud,

dead at twelve, lying in the tomb with Philip
        of Macedon. Think of Sokrates showing Plato

into his cell, refusing escape, waiting after his sip of
        hemlock for cold to rise in his shackled legs.

Think of a dark cave and Plato lost in love.

Eating at Casa Blanca

Eating at Casa Blanca with my pen
        and paper, first I dip

warm bread in olive oil. Here I can
        scribble for an hour

all alone and eat crêpe manicotti

with spinach and drink the flower

of Jasmine Fancy tea. The universe
        is intimate. We're friends.

She drops delicious in this verse.

This evening after I was asked to leave

This evening after I was asked to leave
        Tina's Take-Out where I often eat

(it was 8, closing time) I rolled down my sleeve
        to read a minute more in the light

leaking out the November door. Then walked
        toward my car and there, right

under my feet, three pennies, super novas filled
        with copper souls, showed me

I had friends in the cosmos and I was thrilled.

Through my binoculars

Through my binoculars I see the face
        of God, who is humiliated

to be caught by an atheist. He tries to erase
        my vision, but his powers failed

him and he stands on his head to reduce
        catastrophe. It's as if I nailed

the emperor of Teheran who, if I let him escape
my gaze, might kill me

as he threatened to murder Shahrazad,
the Persian tale teller if she stopped
inventing another night.

Then God takes a deep breath,
swallows black light,

straightens my hump, and his face
holds seven blue oceans in a grape.

What is inside?

What is inside? Down is a lost global blur
where memory lights a cave

of water in a deeper cave. I try to stir
a black sea. I can't,

yet like every slave to birth—if I'm like you—
I float about like an empty soul, ignorant,

which is my tub of hope, waiting for
the waters to be

transparent sky—yet what I say
is exhausted noise,
the throat of the poor.

In his last brief cantos Ezra Pound who wrote
so much bright bunk
was almost silent as he stepped darkly to his boat.

The body is my room

The body is my room, low rent, no lease
       and if the walls collapse

I could skip into the dark night of peace
       impossible. Yet I won't jump.

My room has a window. No door. I bump
       against other rooms and don't slip inside

except for dreams in an ecstatic watery crack
       or in a mouth of garden blue.

Then I wake in sorrow in my sloppy sack.

Despair is a crystal

Despair is a crystal that an artisan ground.
       In it a woman shaped drops

of surprise. I have bribed my way down
       into her bubble and sleep there

poorly, which helps me dream. I take off
       my old-fashioned jacket of worry.

Maybe I'm not that bad? And con my way out.
       Surprise. Time on earth looks good. My friends

suffer long, but I dance on my ball of doubt.

I'm just a man

I'm just a man, which is not unique,
    though this is my first

passage into the mystique
    of consciousness

and time. When my days go, the earth
    won't have time to dress

in black, yet I will have eternity
    to think it over

as I feed a drunken cypress tree.

Presocratics liked atoms

Presocratics like atoms which are
    so tiny only the mind

can see what fixes them together
    in cool fire. Some say strife

is glue for invisible stuff. Pythagoras
    sees a hidden life

in singing numbers, yet by her white dove-
    cot in Mytilene a poet knows

the cosmic force on earth is love.

I don't mean to shock

I don't mean to shock but by the Sierra Nevada
                                    I recall
    a Roman aqueduct

of gold patina that was our *finca's* back wall,
    and in Almuñécar I was so young

I heard the moon stamping her yellow boots
    when she hung

above my heart standing on a lemon hill.
    The moon stripped her panties and glared

her dark crater down for my outrageous thrill.

Nothing wails like the tethered donkey
Donkeys like garbage better than gold.
—Herakleitos

Nothing wails like the tethered donkey through
    the air of Moorish Spain.

He pauses in the middle of his blue
    outrage. On our bench a modest man,

Justo, gypsy friend, sings *soledades* very quiet
                                    like a blind girl
    circling a weathercock. A fan

of olive trees blows old passion on
    a sunless afternoon. But the donkey howls
                            for freedom,
baleful and yearning, a captive prophet in Babylon.

318

Through sunny May in Colorado Springs

Through sunny May in Colorado Springs you leapt
    from the roof of the Sterling Building

to smashing darkness. Dad, since then I've slept
    dreaming us alive. Piece by piece

I sew you back together. In Mexico City
    at the Mountain of Piety you buy ambergris

and diamonds. You give me a silver watch.
    I've pawned my life for you (you gave me mine)

to stand you up again. I dream us and watch.

Honey in the hills

Honey in the hills. I've been happy all day.
    It's love what else

can it be? My armless dead gray
    is orange like Miro.

Women are sorrow with eyes. Women
    cause the rainbow

and infinity. They are sun
    dressed or naked. Feeling crazy orange

is melons in the grass. Breathing is fun.

Please try on my body

Please try

on

my

body who

is dying to dance

in you,

and in joy light let

us

get wet.

The invisible is free

The invisible is free, each atom a salt
as tasty as the Brooklyn Bridge.

Imagine that free vagabond Walt
loafing on it, over blue fish between

the boroughs, bawling at her steel spider web
and her stone. Is the mind a bean

invisible? She is an invisible Buddha yet
no free spirit like Walt whose body,

a bit plump, leaps nimbly with joyous sweat.

I'm no dope. I know

I'm no dope. I know Walt had to take
           the creaky Brooklyn Ferry. Let him feel

a later blast. His friends scorned him as a flake,
           the failed loudman who set type

to print his coarse song, but he sang immune
           to gravity. He kept a penknife to swipe

a piece of wind spirit and like Perseus rose
           over the East River and continent.

Did he fall? He dropped perfect like windless snows

I miss you

I miss you. I am the solitary one.
           I go to movies

alone and eat alone. At one
           a.m. I'm in my office, say

a big goodnight to the all-night janitors
           who know the way

I am, or have become. I miss you. I write
           for you and abhor

this solitude, or love it. I'm not right.

It's good to sleep deep

It's good to sleep deep. At the New York Y
          I take a small cheap room,

a narrow monk bed and no bath. Don't sigh
          for me. I slept well. Then

in the morning I push a flamboyant young black woman
          a few blocks in her wheelchair over puddles
                   through the hopping traffic. When

she finds out I'm a Hoosier she belly laughs at me, a jerk
          from nowhere. Victory at the Y and I fly back

to noplace where my sleep is a miracle at Dunkirk.

Time is life

Time is life. No time is an eternity
          and in no way delicious

since a good meal means a chance to be
          alive and wasteful. I mourn

when a life runs out of nows. It's no tango
          when a friend drops unborn

because her watch stops. Life is time,
          and a drop of blood in my ankle

can knock me cold. In terror I laugh and rhyme.

Deep Down

Deep down I am a good man. But deeper still
        my abscessed tooth pounds and whispers:

You're not good. You're frail, you lie, and I fill
        your brain with pus and pain.

Why must I collapse and mope before my rotting jaw?
        I work like a mule and dance in green rain

for friends. *But you're a klutz!* Go, tooth. I wed
                my soul
        to words, to sweet air of verse, my wacky role

of getting lost for life. *You're an idiot.* Yet way down
        in me I cook a tiny bible. Who am I?

Impermanence, the molar sighs. *You're barely a pronoun.*

Do I know where I'm going?

Do I know where I'm going? Nothing. No.
        I never did, but I stole

time and made friends with Sappho
        and went to her school

in white Mytilene and lay down. We made love
        in her small amphitheater on a cool

parsley night of desire. The Milky Way lay
        a few inches above her Ionic nipples.

Her apples babbled. She won't go away.

My clay soul sat cheerfully pondering

My clay soul sat cheerfully pondering in
          this dipping and bouncing body for nearly

seventy Novembers. Good ride. Now charged with
                    the sin
     of age, I'm guilty and laugh,

stare in the mirror at my blurry face
          (no glasses on) and see a daff-

y youth. Good memory. Yet I can't make my clock
          tick back. Desolate? I'm standing in light,
                hilarious,

and dream of hanging from clouds by my cock.

The air is good this morning

The air is good this morning. It is almost fall.
          I hear this part of Indiana

is a rich flyby for snow geese who sprawl
          their screeching across

the firmament all the way down to Patagonia.
          I breathe like the invisible albatross

off the raging Cape of Good Hope. Multitudes
          of birds are floating in sleep.

We're all breathing eager before winter broods.

Death is so ordinary

Death is so ordinary that when I hear
        a friend has shut her eyes

I'm cowed, bleak, and know that God the cashier
        has thrown another soul

into his dark drawer. We, who still owe
        him one, hurry to scroll

the planet for info and pleasure. I drink
        my slug of Pedro Dome

and tango slow before I too must stink.

A thin man I'm shaking

A thin man I'm shaking. Calm down, calm down.
        I've learned the claw of fear. Am in it.

It holds my head. I hang like a cloth clown
        over the village. If ever a good god

of space or soul would care to cut me loose
        and help me on the ground, show now. Plod

me under the smell of freshness. A thread swings
        me through nights of terror. Pause and be

a good cold morning with ah! bright wings.

To know peace is not all bad

To know peace is not all bad. Peace comes
              like hot sun inside—not death or surrender.

Comes gentle rain, surprise beauty, and hums
              gentle stillness after noisy pain.

Consider the lily on its mountain of spices,
              eaten by deer or quickly slain

by time. Yet lilies are brighter than Solomon's great
                            black tents.
              Their quick cosmic note makes death

take a powder. They glow innocently in lily silence.

Bartleby the scrivener stood all day

Bartleby the scrivener stood all day behind his screen,
              staring at the brick wall outside his window

down on Wall Street. Pallid, thin, unseen,
              the forlorn copyist preferred not to copy or to leave
                    the lawyer's rooms.

Day and night the former Dead Letter Office clerk sat
                  by the banister, locked out,
              until the landlord hustled him up to the Tombs.

There the turnkeys gave him the freedom of a patch
              of grass and the grubman offered food,

but, preferring to be with kings and counselors,

the silent man refused
to dine and soon lay down on the yard to die.

Bartleby is the other side of me,
and though he was a scrivener and the forlorn
ascetic
never acquiesced,

I would still prefer not to be Bartleby.

My father said

My father said to keep my head erect.
I see him now, spiffy on Maine grass with

Blondie. The old photo keeps alive a perfect
couple. They were happy and suffered like

everyone, and died young. Time never took
their agility away. Death got its spike

in first. Tonight let's forget time and laugh and eat
together. In Tibet we met in dream.

Sweet ghosts, I hug you now from my cold sheet.

It is snowing

It is snowing and the big window at the Y
has biblical white plums falling thick

into an old lady's shoes left in a hurry
on the soaked ground when she stepped

into an ice-white ambulance and sirened away
to die. In warm water I'm swimming. It's too wet

to wear a pen, but flesh needs none to recall. I remember
my mother's fun walk, her sleep, her freeze.

Our bodies can't forget the ice of black December.

I was born late

I was born late, too late to be Edith Piaf
or a Cycladic peasant carving stone

for Picasso's eye, and like an old photograph
of an almost arrived tugboat, I miss

the port, blow each deadline. I'm plum late
without excuse. You're right to be pissed

and I swear I'll do better. Tonight maybe
before I sleep. But in wild weakness I still

hope not to show when death sings out for me.

The soul's the rub

The soul's the rub. I can almost rub
my fingers in the milk

of paradise, because I keep a prohibition tub
of cognac and cellos in her

ready to drink or hear if I go twilight dim
and want to leave, to cheer

myself with alien death. The soul can't talk
      but I talk to her

who responds in signs— best is a long walk.

Walk long

Walk long and even when the road is brief
      each step is infinite. Here

in Canada the geese breathe the same arctic grief
      that floats in my unfound soul,

but geese ignore the cold. They're flying pin high
      from gaucho Patagonia. I am a man of coal

smoldering below those fire-eyed birds caught
      in their habit of electricity.

Long or brief I breathe green sky until I clot.

It was a pity I died

It was a pity I died. On my cheap office couch
      I lay down to nap, and dropped sweet

into a delicious orgasmic dream when ouch,
      I felt a twinge in my leg.

A blood missile fired up toward the window
      of eros. NO! I wept. The egg
of thought flew up and landed tenderly
      in a wild garden. I was so glad.

Book in hand, fruit in mouth I walked eternally.

How could I have worried?

How could I have worried? I didn't know
        the way of death. I take my hat off

to her. This night I love her, infinite vertigo,
        we're high, and though jealous God, Señor

of cabaret guitars, took my good father early,
        here we open our white Buick car door

and circle Cycladic skyroads. We're summer wheat,
        don't stop. Sweet and fresh! Yet I fear

I'm writing this and wake on my lone street.

Stepping in the rain

Stepping in cool rain in muggy summer is fun,
        my glasses watery. I never use

an umbrella. Better to bathe in the sky and run
        for cover. This morning I walk.

Water is love. It hugs fish and hermit crabs
        and mammals lick it up. I talk

to each drop holding the fire of India inside
        its splash. Even in the Y pool, love

flows everywhere. I'm swimming to my bride.

330

It's raining in the woods

It's raining in the woods and in my soul.
          That's good, I sorely needed calm.

The rain is everywhere, helps me seem whole
          but I've no soul, just the night word

for soul, a conscious me. Long ago I turned my bed
                    to face the window.
          Rain is beautiful, a billion meditating birds

who make the air hugging the earth the banjo of
          a sky soul quieting thought.

Calmly I sleep and hear the rain pinging wet love.

Deep down I smell the road

Deep down I smell the road the rain the raven
          and I am happy for the light,

all light, the lamp bulb by my bed, lighting Eden
          on the pages of slim hope.

I'm bodied in erotic night: read and float,
          write and doze with thighs, and grope

toward a darkness desolate to see or know.
          There I smell nothing true but

the road the rain the soul the blur the glow.

Full moon, cold white lion

Full moon, cold white lion over the forest line,
        yawns weary of eternity, but I freeze

under her rising jaw fresh on my spine.
        My clothes shiver. In them I've gone

to Puerto Ayacucho in the Amazonas where
        naked Yanomani watch the tundra swan

fly overhead. She is their hot full moon. They cook
        a baby monkey in a big pot of boiling

water, ask me to share a bowl, but I turn north,
        reading snow. Like my emptiness wanting soul

the white beast of stone is a cold bright book.

Love, warm friend waiting in bed

Love, warm friend waiting in bed, I slip in
        and like spoons we curve and hold tear

drops between our chests. Your skin
        and mine talk. I worry, because I'm talking

now through a keyboard and my bed is empty
        (this is just a poem) but I'm stalking

memory and hope. You say *quiet, just come*
        even closer. I squeeze you not to let you go.

amor vincit omnia and like mountains we come.

At l'Hôtel de la Gare du Nord

At l'Hôtel de la Gare du Nord I have no name.
        Do you love me? My train came in from the port

at Le Havre, first night in Paris, in a bistro, the flame
        of the hard boiled eggs, the brass bar. *Un café*

avec du cognac while the beautiful maid in my room
        stole my trousers. I loved her too. No one way

of being at the start of youth. A bible book fat
        or tiny won't tell how, so lift the floor and live.

Death is a bore. Go through the roof at 4 a.m.
        Valentine's Day is a Gnostic trick

to make one happy to exist on this purple gem
        with air around it. Yet breathe, breathe, breathe

until the barman locks up with one quick click.

Some steamed milk

Some steamed milk in a blue and white Italian mug
        in which I drop a bit of cognac
    after midnight to help me

survive the loneliness and desires that will hack
    me awake later. The milk cools off,

her molecules move closer, I cool off too,
    I hear dear Chekhov

humming Bach. They too will chill but I don't care.
What I love is so strong
my fatal clock forgets it is panting

nearly out of breath, punctually, under my chair.

I'm in a state of writing verse

I'm in a state of writing verse. It happens now
almost each day. The faithful pray, I scrawl,

and like Cavafy to his fatal pleasures I say no,
but when night comes or even dawn,

(and I do swear off my habit), the power
of this eros of the hand, of this come-on,

takes over. To her I'm gladly lost. I don't lifeboat
to you (I'd like to), but mumble sounds,

doped by being, inside a pin, and there I float.

The moon is there

The moon is there whether I peer
at her ice mountain eyeball

or not, a nun in her airless sphere,
she is convent cool yet warm

and astonishes. We're never jaded
together. I take her arm

in dark woods or city street. We talk.
She reads me her poems. I clap

and drink her light as we walk and walk.

Happiness is a tomato

Happiness is a tomato with olive oil
    in its red heart

in a plate in the sun, you near on black soil
    or on a wild-rose rock on this Greek

island. Serious joy, it occurs
    at the criminal peak

of weariness or slumping in this chair.
    She is frail as a cat's shriek. She lives on the moon
        right now
        (it's time)

Happiness is fat, a watermelon rolling up a hill.
    She tastes like air.

Delicious Zero   *1998*

Delicious Zero

> That black pearl of Córdoba and Cairo
> was the physician of the soul
> and a lantern contemplating God.
> —Pierre Grange, "On Maimonides (1135-1203)"

We see a statue of Maimonides
on Córdoba's whitewashed stone ghetto floor,
a figure in the walled city, his face
holding deep diagrams by Jew and Moor
of God inside the meditating heart,
an orchard of delicious zero safe
from ordinary death. The dreamer's art
of light is common. I'm a fan, a waif.
This global orphan seeks that mystery dot
of hope, the lie that sanctuaries shine
inside our blur of flesh. In Córdoba
my son and I sitting in the chariot,
insects against the night, drift up to dine
on sky, but angel meat is cold and raw.

A Night in Bethlehem

The angel says to Miryam, "In your womb
there is a child." She's scared, thinking, how can
there be? I haven't known disgrace. My room
is plain. No one has slept with me. No man
has kissed my breasts, and yet I am with child.
That evening after weeping she goes out
and slinks along the streets. Her eyes are wild.
They will not stone her, though the fig trees shout
over the hills: *escape*! Yet she contends,
"I am a barren woman and I feel
no secret love." She is a hill gazelle.
Then Yosef, the young stud, sees her. He bends
to raise her but he rapes her, says, "Don't tell!"
"No lies," she warns. "Wed me so I can heal."

The Last Blind Date

Since I have made a date with death the rat,
she'd better jump me while I'm jogging and
I won't know I am dead, as if a bat
homered me round the world, never to land
except for bouncing me through book stores where
I stock up on the poets whom I love.
I always read at night. In my sky chair
I read Franz Kafka's poems. He soared above
his house down on the Street of the Alchemists,
and fifty years after the rat got him
he scrawled a parable of stars he mixed
with ink to win his trial. But I feel grim
tonight. I broke my date with paradise
to jog in Prague where lovers reek of spice.

Philosopher in the Ghetto

Sketching in the ghetto, Spinoza smokes,
drinks a Dutch beer. Happiness is a chat
with friends. Enemies? He has none. He jokes
about the seen. His invisible is fat
with stars. Love keeps them spinning, and God who
is everywhere is also infinite
and nothing, just like death which isn't true
to life experience and best forgot.
At forty-three the grinder's sick. The good
is what he calmly wants, and he is good,
his friends affirm. He's swallowed too much dust
from grinding lenses. His lungs aren't clean,
time isn't real, and grim with glassy lust
for God as space he fingers the unseen.

Isaac Babel the Day He Was Seized
by NKVD, May 15, 1939, in Pereldelkino
and driven to the Lubyanka prison

Isaac could hardly ride his Cossack horse,
dashing through Poland with the young Red Guard
to free the peasants from their venal lords
and rape a Jew or two. In the back yard
he strangled a black goose on the Shabat
and roasted it, and while the Hasids wept
their flaming tefillin and a tall black hat
sparked holy taste and helped him laugh. He slept
in drunken haylofts with his comrade sheep,
that merry man, Isaac, whose laugh was hot,
who wrote *Red Cavalry* but was a crypto czar
who should be tortured, confessed, tried and shot.
As the policemen threw him in the car
he turned to say, "You guys don't get much sleep."

Keeping Cool When Time Turns Off

Time is the mercy of eternity,
sunny, a drop of light, and all too brief,
for soon my space from that old murder Tree
of Life will wilt as this flesh, like a leaf,
powders to wind. The inner city gone,
its spark of Willis buried, where am I?
If God made death, why care for God? I'm on
a rainbow mountain trek to blind death's eye
and get God off my back so I can stare
at common agonies, enjoying them
as theater of the soul and without fear
in every breath. In time I will not care.
Time will have packed my bags. I'll snip a hem,
unroll my pants, and sip a cosmic beer.

On Board

The stars have us to bed.
—George Herbert

On skyblue sheets we kiss and talk and tent
together through the night. It's beautiful
to dance on clouds until our instrument
of ecstasy is spent; our miracle
of union sleeps so we can also sleep
a tomb of memory and then awake
for more. What do we say? Galaxies keep
on shooting milk through space, our bellies ache
apocalypse, and earthquakes kill the poor
and rich while we are here, humping in blue.
We get up. Time for juice and morning. Though
the body of the world speeds on, its roar
somewhere in us, we stop and joy and screw;
then beach our ship of fools, and pack and go.

Secret Love

When I saw melancholy on the sink
grinning at me, I kept it hid. Why talk
to others or to me of things that link
me to five tiny deer in the snow walk-
ing about for food? We're all the same. You came.
Sappho said it long ago. You came when
the banker told me go to jail. I blame
all that on going blind. Light in my pen
saw you. I dropped the dark and kissed. And you
kissed me. I never thought of ecstasy
standing in a dance hall. For a while we
were happy—thank you white time—and forgot
to grieve. Hello, you said. Grass sang out blue
until our night fell crushing deer and thought.

Cry from the Underworld

Truth is a tyranny stalking me with
his lies. In the unconscious he hides out
where in terrible dialogue the myth
of virtue drags me underground. I shout.
Truth whispers, draining me of courage, and
though I reject the very notion of
a verbal absolute, I cannot stand
his hating face. I pack my things and rove
from me to a geography where I
can laugh and not feel pain. These very words
are muttering abstractions, and truth's way
is personal, a knife through dream. My eye
needs sleep of peace. Turn off the roar. The birds
outside do not sing sweet. There is no day.

Taking a Dive

Daytime I can handle as long as I
don't plop onto the couch and brood
about the night. But when I close an eye
to night there's no escape. One squirming nude
in wet pajamas while some demons bite
patient, watching me tumble down the hill
in Lewiston where I came into light
of milk, then stickball in New York, the thrill
of Casbah lays, and sleep where I am lost.
Sometimes I smile in dreams. The ray of blue
is cheerful like the L.L. Bean blue jeans
I slide the tango in. A call has tossed
me to the demons. Moaning sleep. A few
mad hours until sun climbs and blinds my fiends.

Hot Milk and Brandy

for Gerald Stern

I'm an enthusiast yet it is hard
to step around these rooms I've made look good,
because I face the bed—it's my last card
at night—and sleep, who knows? That darkened wood
wobbles with me and ghosts. I lie in hope
of dropping out the way one dies. Instead
I write some lines in Greek, Cavafy's rope
of courage that he used to fill his bed
with pleasure. Almost no one sees my room
and I am more remote from selling you
a poem. I'd like to, but it's best to write.
That's what I do. I wait like you. The tomb
is empty always . . . no one lives in blue.
I write for us who are nowhere in night.

Looking Each Day from an Empty Head

Morning in my flat is bad sleep. I quit
the pasture of despair, and try to know
again what can't be known. Even a bit
of *who I am* would help. Yet when I'm low,
pain helps; I look more desperately. The list:
why me? why death? what's down there in my mind?
why aren't I cool? The women I have kissed
are more real than me. Worst of all I find
nothing will change even if truth whacks me
straight in the mouth. But maybe it is best.
Knowing? What good is it? Cavafy knew
that too much light would hurt, would lie, would be
unbearable. I laugh, really, and test
my watch. Love runs. My head is blank and blue.

Soul Tree

The soul is not. She's all we have inside,
feeding the working body with a glint
of stars and meditation. When I'm fried
the soul will split. But reason gives no hint
there is a soul. And I agree. I am
not crazy. There's no spirit underskin.
Back to zero. Last night I found a yam
from Easter Island growing deadly in
my brain. It liked the sun and moon of thought,
and while I saw it play with memory
and hope, it laughed at me and split in two.
I guessed it must be Valium time. I ought
to sleep it out. In the yam a soul tree
sang hot with stars as gray depression grew.

In the Night Tower

Should I go back to work tonight? It's late
but there I lose my anguish—others say
I'm full of beans and couldn't guess my plate
of bad food, lowliness, dry soul and clay
pajamas. There I drift away from night
and angry stars, and turn into the salt
of Sodom caves, become a can of white-
wash some old women slap on stone. My fault
is clear and stupid. I am happy and
so tired of sorrow. Think I've had enough
of dark, and in the dark I dance. Idiot?
Why parachute up to black holy land
of stars and pray to pray? Maddening stuff.
Forgive my ecstasy and glowing rot.

Don't Worry. I Won't Be Bitter

To carp. It's not my hope. I'd like to walk
on lettuce in the sky, in my Greek cap
to keep me warm against the wind and clock
that says enough, it's time to sleep and tap
dance in a dream. Don't take my dream away.
It's chocolate. Starting with a breakfast lift
I down the sunjuice and confront the day
with a *Super Delux Aquarelle* gift
sketch book on which I scrawl these words. They make
me dream. Then the electric fix. I look
into a screen and it looks back. After
my eyes give out I nap. Don't worry. Take
my word. Honest. I won't be bitter. This book
of dream, like me, will grin from buried blur.

Needing Peace and Sleep, But with This Heart?

My heart, I mean the meat pounding inside
my ribs, sending blood pissing through my head,
it works and never sleeps, and though I hide
under blue Guatemalan wool, in bed
I'm sad and recite lines I've just made up.
I'm down, I pop a pill, my head is heart
that won't lie angel still. I take a cup
of hot milk fired with cognac and I start
to love a new moon holding up her face.
My heart, you hear my babble. Will you stick
with me? I couldn't know the difference
if you cut out. I'm old and wild and trace
my fires to young Oliver Twist whose trick
was wanting more. I'm cold with no defense.

Poking the Years, 1943

Father and I were scandalously glad
in Mexico. War tore up Europe yet
here were two guys, he fifty, me a bad
fifteen, on double dates all to forget
our fires back home. Walking a midnight street
(where gold and onyx shone behind the glass)
leading to the great Zócalo, our feet
in brand new leather shoes entered the mass
of *la gran Catedral.* The Indians spoke
to us in Spanish, I interpreted
and Dad was proud. The saints were kind. They stared
from their great Asian eyes. A little poke
and Dad saved me from heaven. Wrongly dead
he takes my hand again. He fled, but cared.

Tango Lessons

In Mexico when I had nineteen years,
Marti, my father's widow, living here
behind the *Catedral,* poor, unbitter,
sends me to tango school—"and twenty years
no es nada," sang Gardel. With a soft look
I'm holding my first love and the slum street
where we sleep on the floor; evenings I shake
in the young arms of the professional
girls of the bright dance hall, who bend my arm
and push my legs around the room. Dark, tall
they rub me and I squeeze them. It is right
to burn the globe. Life is a bubble. Our feet
spin through the *ocho,* then glide without harm
across the polished floor, innocent and light.

Winter Orphans in Mexico, 1946

The Spanish civil war, their parents dead,
a troop of refugees poured out of Spain
and docked in Mexico. I found a bed
in a white room on their roof, and got plain
beans, potato tortillas, my cot, all just
for friendship and English. I was a free
orphan like them. On evenings of young lust
I stayed out late, read books all night, a cafê
on Calle Delatrán where whores sat down,
the smells were milky. Manolete came
to town to fight. I didn't go, but sold
my blood, bought a white jacket, went downtown
on a first date. We danced and knew no shame.
Back on my orphan cot we rode the bull.

French Cake in Mexico, 1946

The year I sleep up on the roof in a
room I climb to by outdoor ladder, sun
wakes the snow volcanos Popo and his La-
dy Ixtacihuatl, who gleams at dawn.
Our orphanage has bean soup but I starve
for sweets, and when Paco takes me to eat
at a French dame's elegant digs I cave
in love for Françoise, her fat crêpes, her feet
in braces up to her knees. Smiling she urges
platters of cream cakes all afternoon on us
& plays Offenbach's *La Gaité Parisienne*.
I fall for older women. Young blood surged
between my virgin legs. Home on the bus,
squashed, cold, I ache for her sweet oxygen.

What It's Like to Burn at Nineteen, Read Dos Passos and Hemingway, and Dream of Women

At the Benjamin Franklin Library
I find hot books to keep me reading till
the dawn. Once through an art-class door I see
a naked woman posing. I freeze still
on the staircase. Women are mystical
earth beings, the alien sun in soul or in
the air where I can spoof with them. Yet all
my dreams are ignorance. I've never been
in bed with mystery. An older friend
(I'm young for her) tells me to save my juice,
she knows a *chica* on her floor who'd sleep
with me. No. Yet soon in blue Vera Cruz
the sheets of a rented room burn. We blend
our virgin thighs. Fishing is fun and deep.

Dancing Flamenco Alegrías in Franco Spain, 1961

In the basement of a building in Madrid
down in the Rastro, I opened the door
to greet maestro Diego Marín. Timid
(I was no good), I kicked the echo floor
with my tight boots, wildly stamping my feet
in the damp afternoon. A gypsy grinned
at me. Her hair was dagger tight. My beat
was bad. Diego Marín like a black wind
battering the olive trees—he'd lost a foot
to quick gangrene—yelled at me with contempt.
I stamped and clapped but had no grace. He put
me next to his good leg and rapped the wood
under his heel, pounding the stars. I dreamt
I was on Mars, cantering in a stone wood.

349

Occurring with Friends
Miguel Hernández (1910-1942)
Antonio Machado (1875-1939)

My best friends died before I was. But they
wake me almost every evening. Tonight
I talk with young Miguel Hernández. His ray
of darkness looks at cockroaches and light
of paper dolls he cuts out for his son
while he sags in fresh tubercular milk
coughed out in his jail cell that has no sun.
He's dead at thirty-two but I still drink
from his cup and from far Machado snow.
Miguel and don Antonio. We talk
till dawn. They save me and I steal their blur,
their heart, their skill. "Enough," friends tell me. "No.
Don't rob their tombs." How happy when I walk,
robbing Machado and Miguel. Then we occur.

Falling Off the Earth

On this ordinary night after I go
to sleep, it is odd that I have slipped off
the earth. Shitty mistake and I don't know
how it happened. I didn't even cough,
shiver or ache. Being unprepared I feel
cheated, yet it has occurred to a world
of folks. How odd not to wake, yet I steal
hours from the angel of death, and now curled
in my black pearl of nothingness I bitch
about this mess. Frankly, something is wrong.
I have a bunch to do (for one, I'd like to write
this poem), settle my heart with a sweet throng
of souls, and even say goodbye. The light
is out. I'm off. Don't drop me in a ditch!

Rattling through the Afternoon, Sad to See
the Tango Man Go Limp

I rattled through the afternoon when I
found out that WB was gone for good,
meaning I'd never look into his eye
and see him dance with Dante in the wood
of melancholy. I made him this room
where we holed up. I didn't miss him. No,
he was a weakling with a prison broom
to meet the trash of age, the words, the glow
of brandy and ice cream he danced with on
a Turkish rug. He died before he took
his art on tour. A lonely man can laugh
like a growl plane in mountain night. Till dawn
he wrote spiked to his chair. I heard him cough,
mutter and groan, and die into this book.

Pilots of Spirit

Plotinos and Spinoza have dropped in
for a cookout. They are fun guys and not
at all pompous or cold. Just imagine
these pilots of the soul (who mapped the lot
of that country below the blur that no
one sees) having a ball with Piazzo-
la, maybe picking up a step or two
of La Plata tango. The seen is untrue,
but union of two lovers is a copy
of union of the soul and light. Sloppy
and drunk on the illumination of
hot dogs and cokes, my pals of secret things
are circling down to the airstrip of love
and root for me to put on the soul's wings

Je suis bien triste as it gets dark on a hill
where I look out into the heart of a woman

There is a sadness in the physical.
A bad birth causes a brain hemorrhage
or memory slips away like a child's ball
over a cliff, or flesh is joy, my page
wings in the attic where I sit with time
remembering the tons of rain I drop
into the heart of a woman. Her name
is lost. I love her madly. She should chop
me up. Afternoon of a fawn. You see,
no spirit here, but I walk to the edge
of madness and nostalgically I kiss
her. We are waiting. I have been. The sea
crashed all night under our window; hiss
of Greek winds. Laugh at this fool in his beds.

I Knew a Woman with One Breast

I knew a woman with one breast and we
spent a fresh night together in a tent
at a summer Blue Grass festival. She
invited me in. Bean Blossom. We went
dancing into darkness on the hard grass.
I balanced on her chest, tilting into
our mystery. She was milk. Full breast and ass
on the damp delirious ground. A few
seconds of joy and earth till the dawn air
when we took down the tent and she went back
up north. She was a botanical artist
for text books, sent me letters and a sack
of dry lilies. She lost her other breast.
Her last letter to me held her last hair.

Dark Afternoons in the Austere Music Room
at the Back of the Old Bowdoin Chapel
Where in 1944 I floated in the Fin-de-Siecle Song

College days. Just sixteen. Why was I there
so soon? My roommate fell in love with me.
I couldn't help him. Through north twilight air,
up in the gray stone tower, plump Timothy
hammered the chapel chimes, a one man band.
Gongs washed the violet campus. Eager, I
climbed up to the high music room to stand
like a snow ghost, lie on the floor, and die
hearing Debussy's *Claire de Lune*, Verlaine,
Votre âme est un paysage choisi.[1] Douce France
in Maine. I skipped dinner and through the night
my soul loved scratchy 78s. My pen
was not yet born to melody, to dance
on water, but I soaked in Gallic light.

Strange to Be 70

Not me. I'm just a squirt or infantile.
You may be old. Rilke was dead the year
before my birth and he died young. I smile
at my mistake. I like that atmosphere
of Prague, the poets, Jews, and Kafka whom
I chat with every day. He tells those strange
brief parables, his Testament. His room
on the Street of the Alchemists I change
for mine. We all are ghosts, so why give me
an age? You win, I am not Paracel-
sus, who can make a fireplace give birth
to sea carnations, yet one century
from now I'll get to know new friends in hell
and write deep memoirs under the blue earth.

---

[1] Your soul is a chosen landscape.

Creating God

Until they get to the Phoenician coast,
pushing their sheep and goats, eating the weeds
and Asian desert plants, some times a roast
of fresh gazelle, they count by fingering beads
and feed their many gods, their Elohim,[2]
with precious meat. Avram listens to one
of them, Yahweh, pausing before his scream
of fire: "Take a stone, tear your penis. Your son
Yitzhak will live." And with that covenant
his children roam to Egypt, lugging stone,
escape to Zion where in black tents a few,
weary of deities, invent
a Nameless one high in the sky alone.
So Jews create a God who makes the Jew.

Grayhaired Man at a Table Scribbling on a Napkin

According to Saint Thomas, angels are
pure spirit or intelligences just
like God or ghosts. They pause under a star,
above a cloud, and there they smile and lust
for females. "A good woman ought to veil
her head," Paul warns, "because of angels." I
should veil my soul since I'm a lonely male
and weak before a woman floating by.
I look for safety in the restaurants
where bad cooks (without women) sit like me
alone and read. I read and sometimes write
about an angel who has seen my haunts
and walks in, fallen in felicity.
I sit in dark, smelling her skin of light.

---

2 Elohim, meaning Gods, is the plural of Eloah, God. Hebrew Genesis
begins, *bereshit bara elohim et ha-shamayim ve-et ha-aretz,* which is
literally "In the beginning created Gods the heavens and the earth."

Old Man with a Cigarette

When I see an old man walking the street,
troubled by his gray depths, waiting for time
to solve or heal the facts of age, I eat
my tongue and lock my hope. I will not rhyme
his failure and gray hair with mine, and yet
not Sherlock Holmes of Baker Street or God
of Israel, Rome or Mecca ever let
this fading human win a round. I nod
to him. He doesn't see me cruising by
in my Accord. His eyes fatally soak
up nowhere air. He looks grimly alone,
smoldering with his cigarette. Goodbye.
I face the mirror and enjoy my bone
with happy flesh on it. We both are smoke.

What Can One Person Do on Earth?

My brother tried, then killed himself. I'd like
to help but lack an outfit. One of me,
what good am I? The Quakers simply hike
through poor pueblos, give free shots and worry
about crucified mermaids. I'm an insect man
who's got a memory and my heart is big.
I try to serve with words. Don't laugh. This clan
of artists is a mob. We do our gig
and hope, but Quakers know I'm impotent
compared to them. A sardine factory nun
in Lapland I could be, sharing her long night
of peace after a day of work. I'm sent
by none—my French nun was—I love the sun
and take your hand until there is no light.

Once by a German Beer Garden

Once by bright beer gardens in Heidelberg
we drove into the forest. It was "black,"
they told us. Then tender as an iceberg
of acid rain, it melted; I look back
and it's alive and we are still cheerful.
My heart is hot with bedroom rain and sin,
good sign of wonder. I sat with a bull
in Soria to watch it loaf, have always been
a vagabond and seldom own the bed
I sleep in. Since the algebra of day
dumbs me, I stray a black forest of light
with you, and flop and bounce up happy (not dead
like burning Irish lads), and rob a way
to oblivion and algebra of night.

You and I on Earth

We are floating around
the sun because of a
big bang. Here on blue ground
we wake just for a day
and you are delicate,
a being who occurs here
floating with me, a fit
of beauty. When I fear
the plunge to zero—no
tango or breath—you pinch
me, save me with a kiss
of darkness, and we know
a night of love and clinch
like boxers soaked in bliss.

BOOKS BY WILLIS BARNSTONE

POETRY

Poems of Exchange   1951

From This White Island   1960

Antijournal   1969

New Faces of China   (poems & photographs)   1972

China Poems   1976

Stickball on 88th Street   1978

Overheard   1979

A Snow Salmon Reached the Andes Lake   1980

The Alphabet of Night   1984

Five A.M. in Beijing   1987

Funny Ways of Staying Alive   (poems & drawings)   1993

The Secret Reader • 501 Sonnets   1996

TRANSLATIONS

Eighty Poems of Antonio Machado.   Introduction by John Dos Passos;
   Reminiscence by Juan Ramón Jiménez   1959

The Other Alexander: Greek novel by Margarita Literati.   Foreword by
   Albert Camus.   (with Helle Tzalopoulou Barnstone)   1959
   Greek Lyric Poetry   1961

Physiologus Theobaldi Episcopi   Bishop Theobald's Bestiary.   Lithographs
   by Rudy Pozzatti   1964

Sappho: Poems in the Original Greek with a Translation   1965

The Poems of Saint John of the Cross   1968

The Song of Songs   1970

The Poems of Mao Tse-Tung   (with Ko Ching-Po)   1972

My Voice Because of You: Pedro Salinas.   Preface by Jorge Guillén   1976

The Unknown Light: Poems of Fray Luis de León   1979

A Bird of Paper: Poems of Vicente Aleixandre.   Preface by
   Vicente Aleixandre   (with David Garrison)   1982

Laughing Lost in the Mountains: Poems of Wang Wei (with Tony
     Barnstone and Xu Haixin)   1991
     Six Masters of the Spanish Sonnet   1993
To Touch the Sky   1998
The New Testament: Four Gospels & Apocalypse. Afterword by
     Harold Bloom   1999

MEMOIR
With Borges on an Ordinary Evening in Buenos Aires   1993
Sunday Morning in Fascist Spain: A European Memoir (1948-1953)
1995

LITERARY CRITICISM
The Poetics of Ecstasy: From Sappho to Borges   1983
The Poetics of Translation: History, Theory, Practice   1993

ANTHOLOGIES / EDITIONS
Rinconete and Cortadillo by Miguel de Cervantes (with Hugh Harter)
1959
Modern European Poetry   1967
Spanish Poetry from Its Beginnings through the Nineteenth Century
1970
Eighteen Texts: Writings by Contemporary Greek Authors (with
     Edmund Keeley)   1973
The New Spoon River by Edgar Lee Masters   1973
Concrete Poetry: A World View (with Mary Ellen Solt)   1974
A Book of Women Poets from Antiquity to Now (with Aliki Barnstone)
1980
Borges at Eighty: Conversations   1982
The Other Bible: Ancient Alternative Scriptures   1984
The Literatures of Asia, Africa, and Latin America (with
     Tony Barnstone) 1998